IN M

Dr. M. T

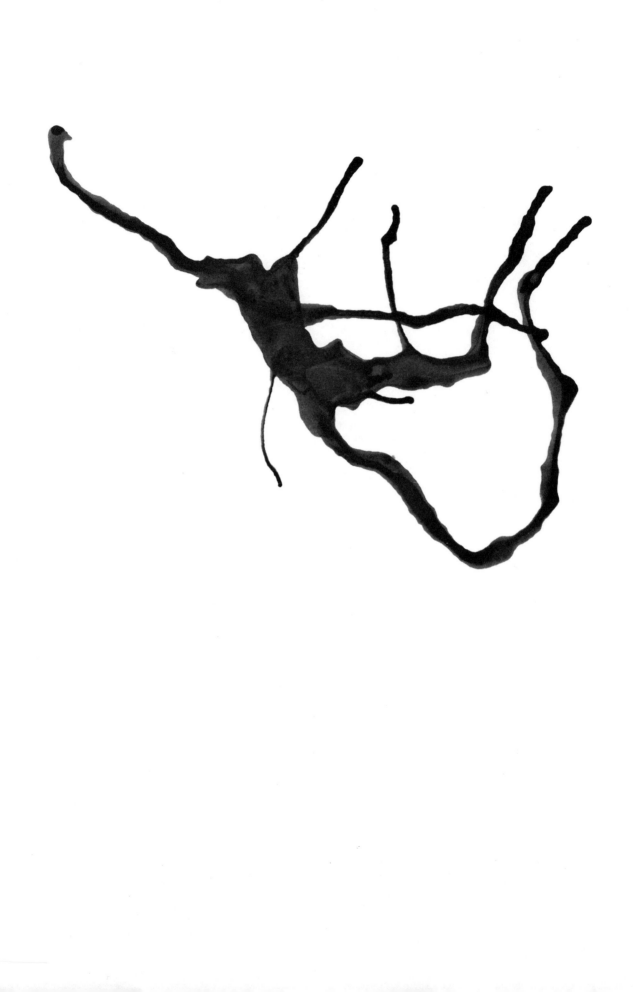

JAMES F. O'BRIEN

design by accident

Dover Publications, Inc., New York

Published in Canada by General Publishing Company, Ltd., 30 Lesmill Road, Don Mills, Toronto, Ontario.

Published in the United Kingdom by Constable and Company, Ltd., 10 Orange Street, London WC 2.

Design by Accident is a new work, first published by Dover Publications, Inc., in 1968.

Standard Book Number: 486-21942-9
LIBRARY OF CONGRESS CATALOG CARD NUMBER: 68-10779

Manufactured in the United States of America
Dover Publications, Inc.
180 Varick Street
New York, N. Y. 10014

Chance is beloved of Art, and Art of Chance.

Agathon, fragments (c. 415 B.C.), quoted by Aristotle.

contents

introduction 1

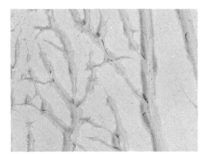

tree forms

Trunks and Branches Formed by the Movement

of Pigments and Liquids

7

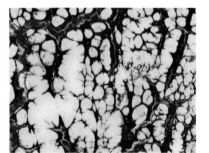

cracks and crackle

Layers in Tension

31

crawl

Rejection of Paint by an Incompatible Surface

53

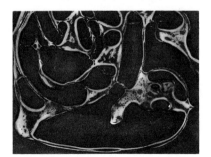

drip, dribble, drop

Pollock's Discovery and Random Patterns

71

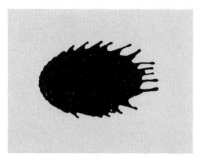

splash and run

Designs Formed by Vigorous Impact and Gravity

91

flow and swirl

"Marble Effect"

121

wrinkles and folds

Folding and Bending of Surfaces

137

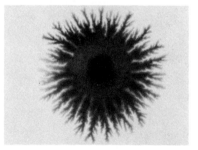

flowers

Patterns Formed by Drops of Pigment on a Coated
Surface

163

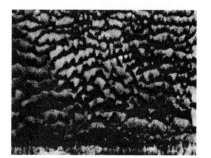

miscellany   181

materials and equipment   210

Color plates follow page 88

Fig. 1.

Fig. 2.

Fig. 3.

Fig. 5.

Fig. 6.

Fig. 4.

Fig. 7.

Fig. 8.

introduction

The man chiefly responsible for the beginning of mechanical picture making, Louis Jacques Mandé Daguerre (1789–1851), was an artist in search of new visual effects. In one of his early efforts, he applied paint to both sides of a translucent canvas and illuminated it from the back, creating an unusual effect like real sunlight. Such experiments increased his interest in finding mechanical devices applicable to picture making and led to collaboration with a French physicist. Together they developed a technique of producing images on metal plates, later known as daguerreotype (Fig. 9). They could not have guessed what a flood of pictures would follow. ■ Today we are deluged with lifelike photographs, thanks to our sophisticated cameras and the developments in high-speed printing, moving pictures, and television. Artists have reacted to this in different ways. ■ Some have accepted the camera as a device for producing pictures of great beauty and sensitivity, as anyone can testify who has seen the exhibit or volume of photographs edited by Edward Steichen, *The Family of Man.* ■ Salvador Dali has created with pigments photograph-like paintings of the dream world that the camera can never see. Other artists have revolted completely against the realistic camera-type image, and have tried to eliminate it totally from their canvases. Jackson Pollock was one of the best-known contemporary artists who have been successful at the elimination of the photographic image. His drips and dribbles made accidental shapes and patterns on canvas that are a delight to the eye, and the simple way he achieved them was a stroke of cleverness that was the astonishment and envy of the art world. ■ In the retreat from the realistic image, things that were at one time considered to be only the *ingredients* have become the *subject matter* of paintings for many artists. Composition, color, tonal values, the way paint is applied, even the materials themselves, are acceptable subjects. With Pollock, the subject was the paint itself and the interesting way it arranged itself into globs, drips, and dribbles, wind-

Fig. 1: Sand oozing down the side of dune. □ **Fig. 2:** Contour marks in wind-swept sand.
Fig. 3: Pebbles on beach. □ **Fig. 4:** "Wind waves" in the sand, Nags Head, N. C.
Fig. 5: Sand waves. □ **Fig. 6:** Sand "erosion" on the side of a dune. □ **Fig. 7:** Designs left in sand by retreating tide. □ **Fig. 8:** Cracks on mud flat. Photos by author.

1

ing and curving its way over the surface of the canvas with minimal control by the artist. Other painters seek new materials, new shapes, new forms, new and different ways of applying paint. They spray, stipple, dribble, squirt, blow, dab, shoot, and scrape on the paint, hoping for a glimpse of the illusive new and different approach. ■ This drive for newness in technique, in shapes, in materials, is quite compatible with contemporary thinking. Researchers discovering new, basic knowledge, and scientist-engineers applying the new knowledge to achieve breakthroughs which result in new processes and products, create a climate which makes the artist's experiments widely acceptable. That an artist should seek new discoveries on canvas in the realm of self-expression seems not too unusual. ■ Nature, the artist's inexhaustible source of inspiration, in its most elemental location, the seashore, demonstrates through a combination of natural forces and materials a great variety of forms which occur throughout the natural world. When the ocean tides begin to ebb, the returning waters leave behind puddles and ponds whose outlines assume graceful *free-form* shapes (Fig. 10). Water trickling back to the ocean traces miniature rivers and deltas on the surface of the sand which also resemble a tree with innumerable branches, twigs, and forks. The wave pattern of the ocean itself is imitated in the wavy wet sand. Dried mud duplicates, on a larger scale, the crackle so prized on certain types of ceramic ware. Some puddles left behind by the tide have a little scum on the surface which swirls and turns in graceful lines as the wind blows across its surface, and a design of marble-like character appears. The endless variety of sky effects—clouds, sunlight, and shade, along with the moods of the ocean—create ever-changing shapes, colors, and forms, which have always given the seashore a magnetic power that attracts most of us, and artists in particular (Figs. 1–8). ■ The intention of this book is to examine natural forms occurring in *accidental effects* that are produced not by the artist, but by elemental forces at work on the pigments—very much like the accidental effects produced at the seashore by the action of gravity, heat, cold, waves, and the action of wind on water, sand, mud, and rocks. Some of the designs produced are simply the result of applying pigments in a particular way. Others result from bringing certain materials together so they react with each other. All the different designs and shapes obtained are the result of natural forces and physical laws. Admittedly, the artist

2

prepares conditions which are favorable for producing the accidental effects, but he does not have complete control over the end result. Variations in temperature, materials, and humidity play a large and uncertain role in making some of them. Of what use are the designs? They are certainly not paintings in themselves, but do contain ideas that can be useful to artists, designers, decorators, and photographers. All of them can be produced quite easily and with simple materials, as described in the accompanying text. ■ The illustrations were not prepared in a scientific way; that is to say, not every possible variation of accidental design was examined, and most of them are simply ideas that were stumbled onto

Fig. 9: Daguerreotype portrait of August Belmont. Library of Congress.

while the author was carrying out commercial art assignments, drafting and sign-painting jobs, or painting pictures. ■ In some cases, a photographic enlargement of a section of a design is shown along with the original design, if it has particularly interesting characteristics. Sometimes a variation of the same design is shown or the reverse is illustrated ("reverse" meaning white on black as opposed to black on white). Most of the originals of the designs reproduced here were done in black and white simply because they photograph and reproduce the original more faithfully than color. Obviously, endless variations in color are possible, the only limitation being the imagination of the artist. The designs illustrated and the

Fig. 10: Scene at Nags Head, N. C., near Jockey Ridge. Photo by author.

methods and techniques used to achieve them are by no means all that are possible, but they may intrigue the reader into doing some exploring on his own. ■ In the act of making the various designs and shapes shown in this book, the artist cannot but be impressed by their universal, all-permeating character, how they occur throughout the natural world in completely unrelated living organisms, as well as in inanimate things. Another fact also becomes apparent: No matter how the artist tries to escape from images of real things, the human mind seems to insist on trying to see realistic images in designs that are themselves an attempt to flee from realism.

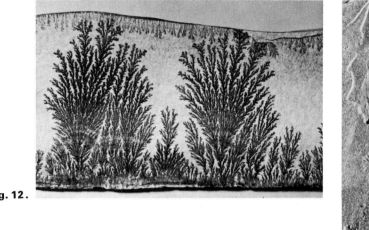

Fig. 12.

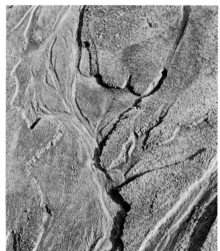

Fig. 11.

Fig. 14.

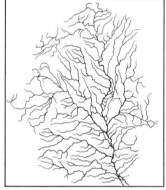

Fig. 13.

Fig. 15.

tree
forms Trunks and Branches Formed
by the Movement of Pigments and Liquids

In ancient times the tree was an object to worship in religious rites. The subject matter of innumerable landscape drawings and paintings, its beauty is undisputed. It is an efficient design for connecting widely separated points with a central stem or trunk. Throughout the natural world we find it, in nervous or circulatory systems of animals, in plants, river systems, deltas, and in the heart of a mineral, the fern agate. ■ One of the methods described in this section for producing tree forms is very much like the process that takes place in nature in the development of rivers and deltas. Watered-down poster color is applied to a non-absorbent surface that is held at an angle so that the liquid will flow downward. As the water in the paint flows to one end of the panel it deposits the heavier particles of pigment on the panel and forms miniature streams and rivers that join to form others of increasing size. ■ Another method also uses the movement of pigmented liquids to produce the tree form. Two pieces of cardboard of the same size are coated with a thick layer of paint. The still-wet surfaces are pressed firmly together, then, held in such a way that the thumbnails can be inserted between the boards at one end, they are quickly pulled apart as if opening a book. As the cardboards are separated, a tug-of-war between the paint particles which adhere to them and the paint particles which cohere with each other causes the paint to move across the surface of the panels, forming a delicate pattern of ribs and ridges with plant-like shape. The intricacy and character of the design vary with the type of paint, the consistency of the ingredients, the flexibility of the cardboard, and the speed with which the panels are pulled apart.

Fig. 11: Sand delta. □ **Fig. 12:** Pyrolusite dendrites, a form of fern agate. Smithsonian Institution photo. □ **Fig. 13:** Amazon River and tributaries. □ **Fig. 14:** Eroded clay bank. **Fig. 15:** Tree in field near Rockville, Maryland. Photos for Figs. 11, 14 and 15 by author.

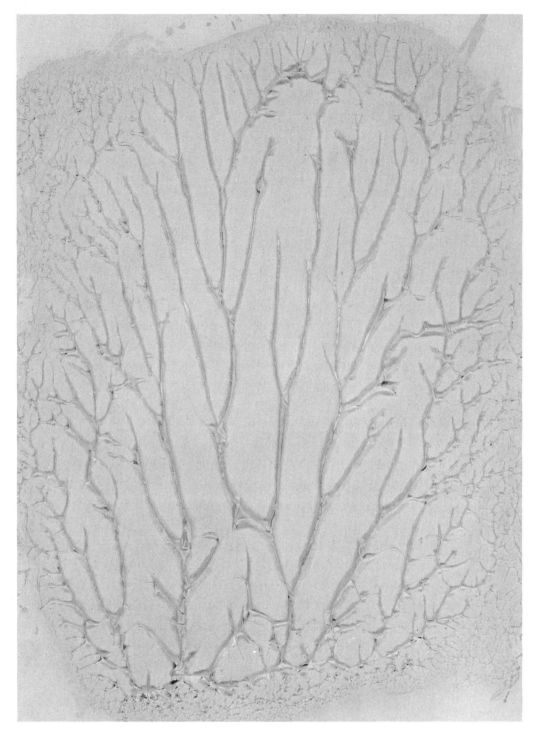

1. With a palette knife apply a thick coat of Grumbacher's MG Quick-Drying White to both surfaces of two illustration board panels, both the same size. Press them face to face firmly, then put your fingernails between the boards at one end and pull them quickly apart, forming the design.

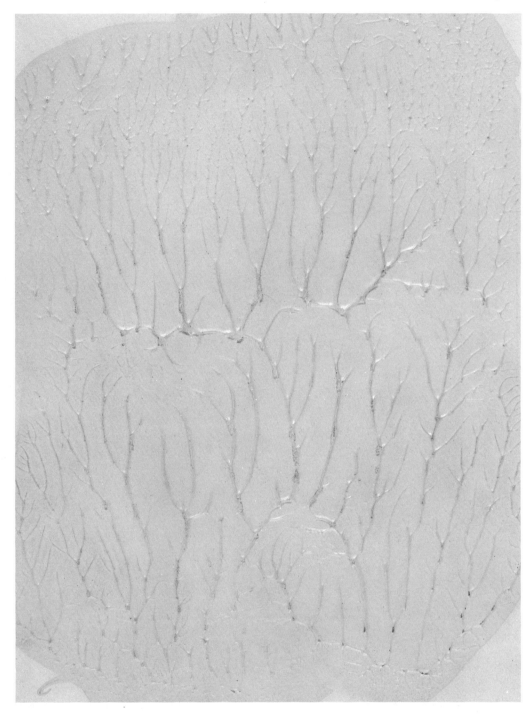

2. Proceed exactly as in the previous demonstration, but thin the MG White with some odorless thinner or turpentine. The ridges or veins will be finer and more numerous.

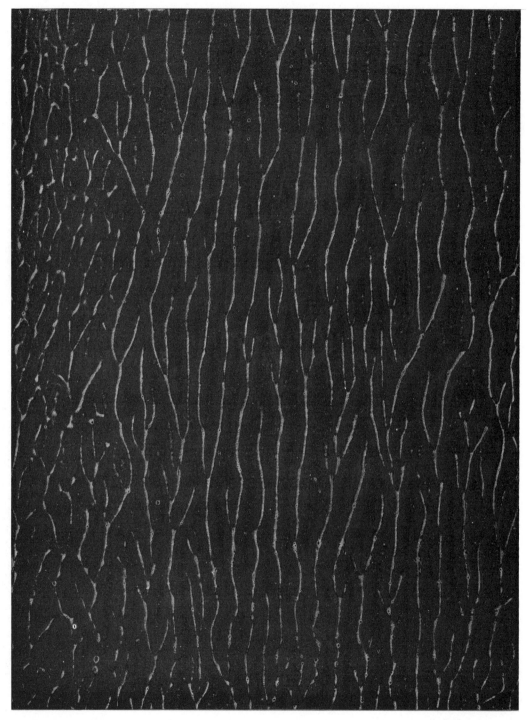

3. MG White is slightly thinned, then applied to the illustration board with a paint-roller applicator of the type used for painting walls. After thoroughly drying, a coat of black enamel spray is applied. When the enamel dries, sand lightly with fine sandpaper.

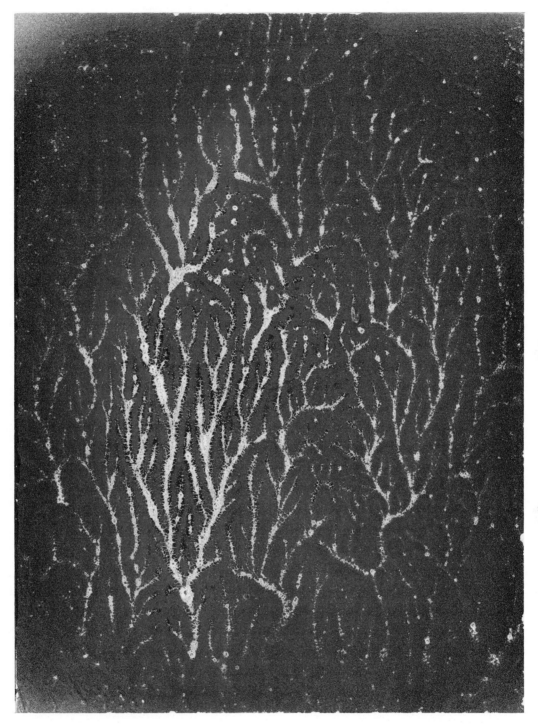

4. Brush a thick coat of white poster color onto two pieces of illustration board, both the same size. Press firmly together, place fingernails in the crack between the two boards at one end, then pull them quickly apart. Lay them flat and allow to dry for at least one hour. Spray on a thick coat of black poster color or black enamel. When completely dry, sand lightly with very fine sandpaper until the tree form appears.

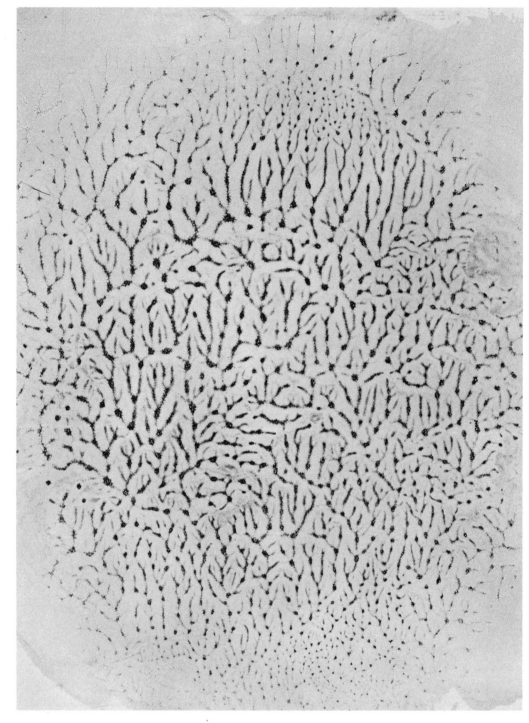

5. Proceed exactly as for Design 4, but use black showcard color on the two boards before pressing them together. Spray them with white, after the first black coat has dried, then sand lightly.

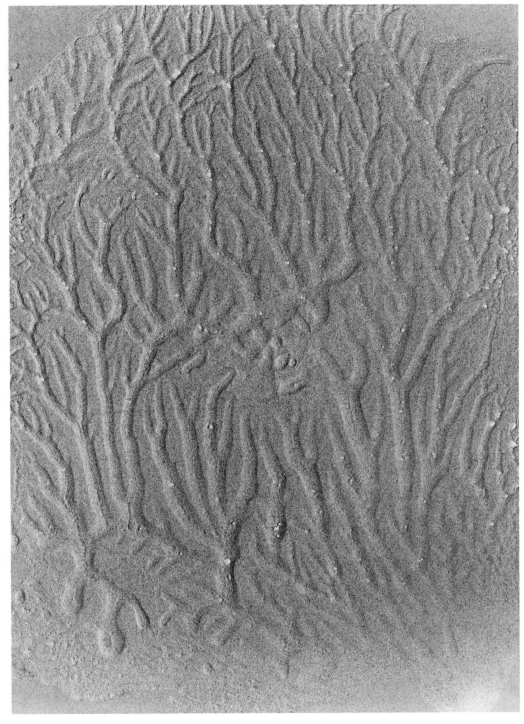

13

tree forms

6. Apply a thick coat of white poster color to two pieces of illustration board, same size. Press together, face to face. Pull apart, as in previous demonstration. When dry, airbrush lightly with black poster color, spraying directly *across the surface*, parallel to the surface of the board. This illustration was sprayed from right to left.

14

tree forms

7. Coat a piece of illustration board with clear lacquer, or spray with white enamel, to get a pure white, waterproof surface. Allow to dry for about ½ hour. Place the panel in a sink, resting one short end on a wooden block or some other support about 2″ high. Using a clean brush about ½″ wide, brush water over the surface, dipping the brush in a little soap or detergent, so the water will not be repelled by the waterproof surface. Put 2 tablespoons of black showcard color into a cup, add 10 tablespoons of water, and mix thoroughly. Brush the surface of the wet panel with the mixture, allowing it to run down the tilted surface. Brush more paint-water across the upper edge of the panel, again allowing it to run down the surface. Repeat about 5 times, brushing only across the upper edge of the panel. Leave the panel in the sink for about 1 hour. After drying over-night, spray the design with fixative.

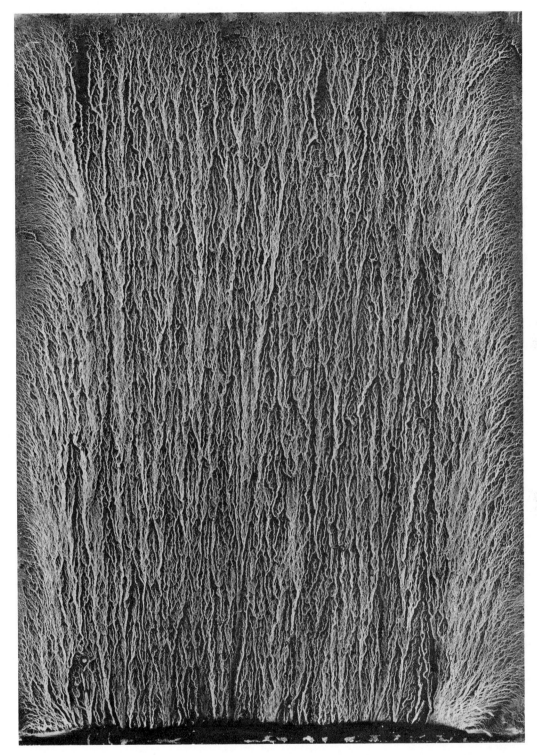

15

tree forms

8. Proceed as for Design 7, except that the panel should be kept in an almost vertical position until the design has formed and has begun to dry.

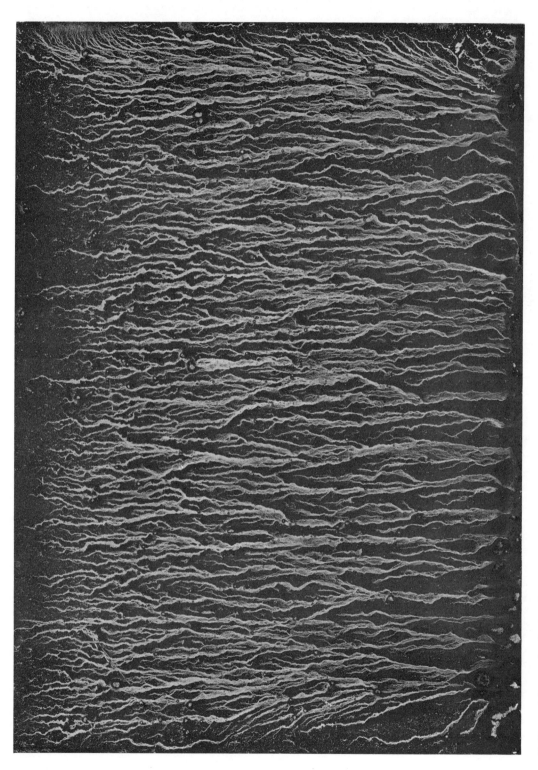

9. Proceed just as for Design 7, on a panel previously painted with lacquer or sprayed with enamel, but instead of brushing the mixture only across the upper edge of the wet panel, brush it straight down from the higher edge to the lower edge, in many strokes, parallel to the sides. Repeat a few times, then leave the panel to form its own design by the movement of the paint and water.

10. Proceed as for Design 7, but rest the panel at a very slight angle, with one end only ½" above the other, until the design has formed.

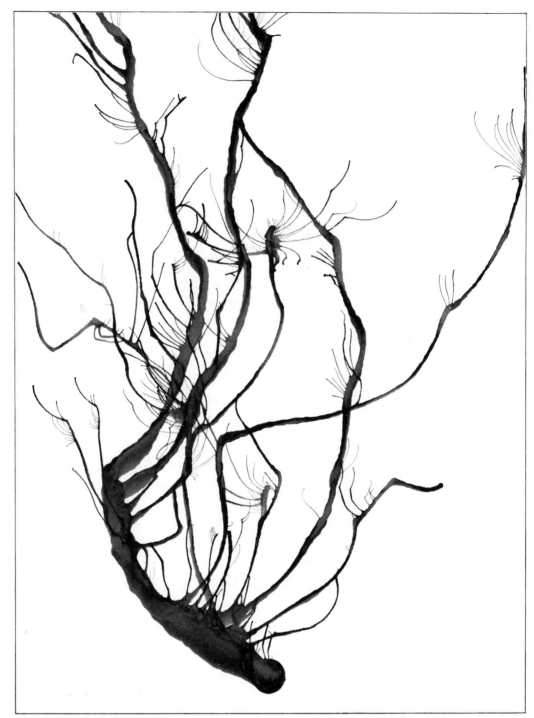

11. Place four drops of India ink about one inch from the bottom of the panel. Using an air brush with no ink in the paint cup, hold the air brush nozzle at an angle of about 30° to the surface, and blow air in an upward direction from the bottom of the panel to the top. Hold the nozzle very close to the surface, always blowing in an upward direction, until every little puddle is dry. The resulting shapes are often like an Oriental artist's version of a tree branch.

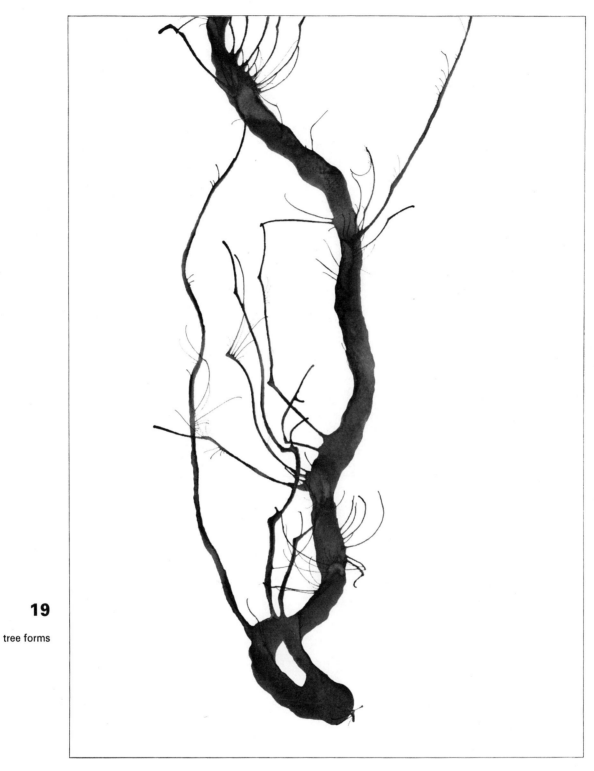

12. Variation of Design 11.

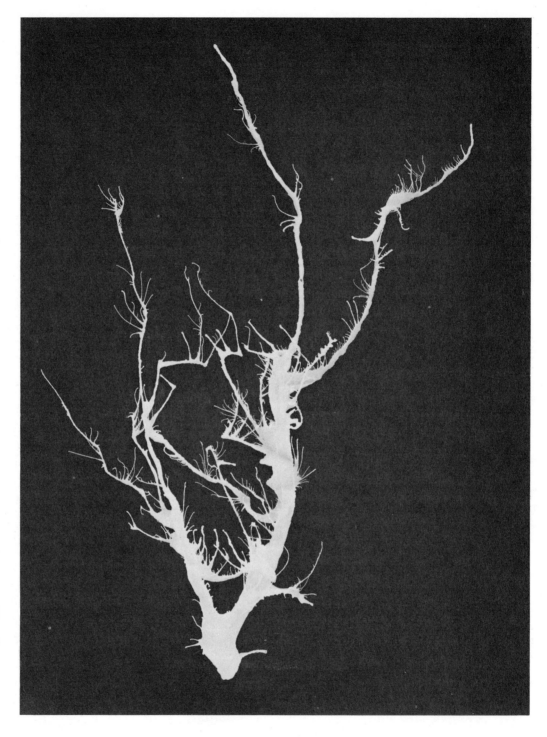

13. Use the same procedure as for Design 11, but use Johnston's Special Grade White ink on black paper.

14. Variation of Design 13.

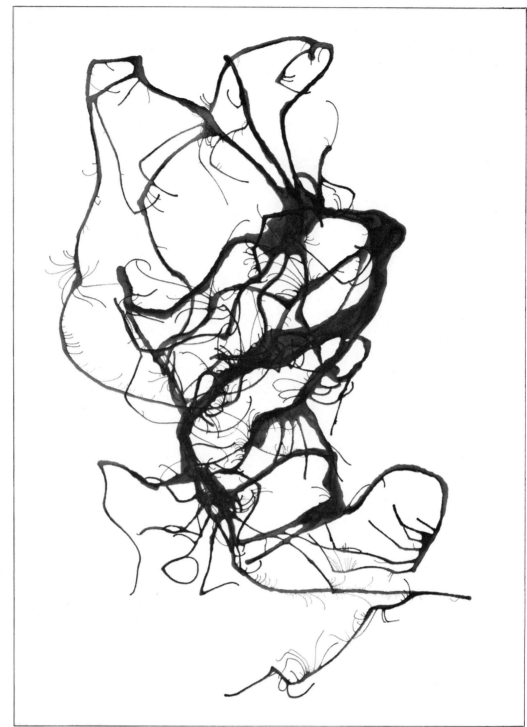

15. Four drops of India ink are placed in the center of the illustration board. Using an air brush, with 25 lbs. pressure, but no ink in the paint cup, blow air on the ink puddle, causing it to separate and branch out.

Hold the nozzle very close to the surface of the panel, blowing on each puddle of ink as it moves across the surface, until the whole area is dry. Branches and limbs will form in unexpected directions.

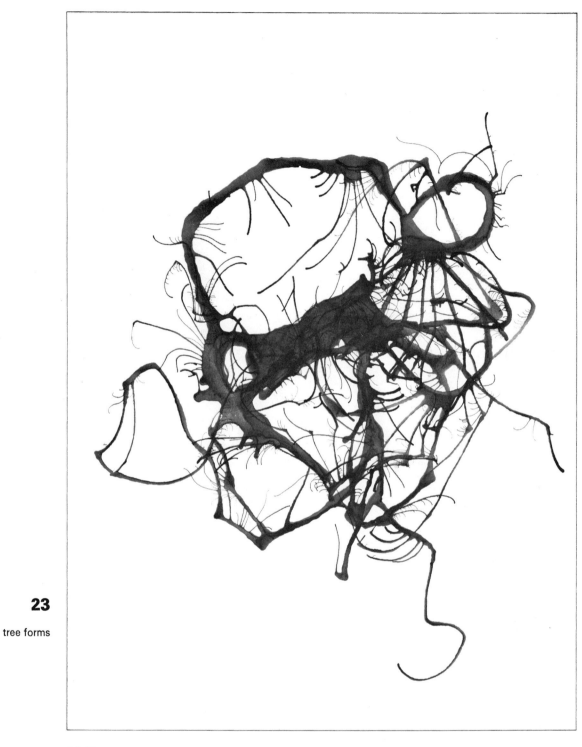

23

tree forms

16. Variation of Design 15.

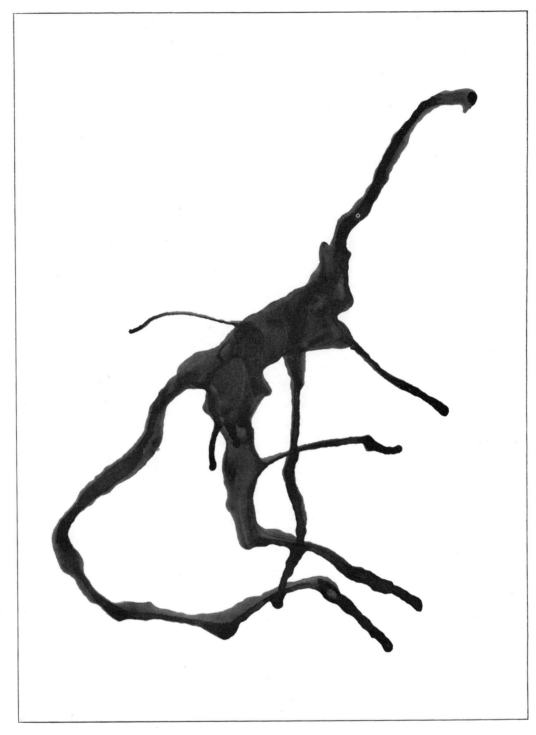

17. Place four drops of India ink in the center of the panel. Using an air brush with no ink in the cup and 25 lbs. pressure, blow air down vertically on the puddle of ink, keeping the nozzle about four inches from the surface. As the ink begins to move and form "arms," continue to blow on the puddles, still keeping at least four inches from the surface. Allow to dry.

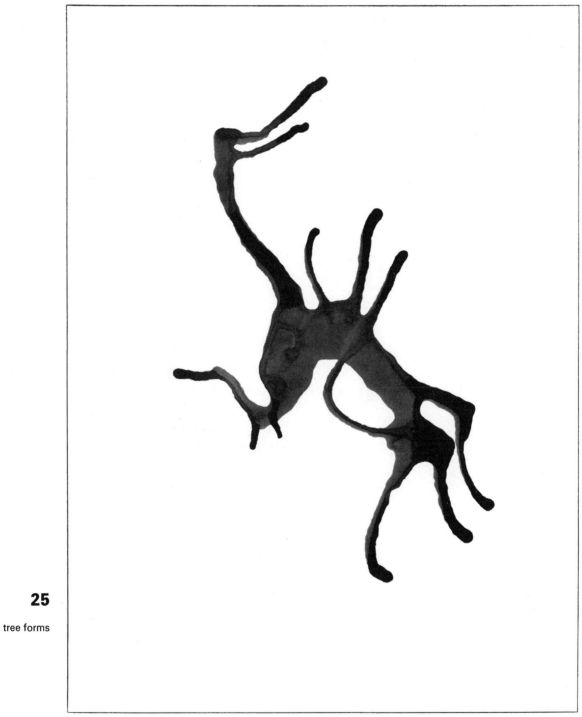

18. Variation of Design 17.

19. Take the same steps as for Color Plate A (opposite page 88), rubbing the surface with yellow crayon. Use blue, blue-green, green, yellow-green crayons; scrape them onto the surface and use the heat lamp as before.

20. With the fingers, spread a thin coat of Elmer's Glue-All over the surface of two equal-size pieces of illustration board. Place them face to face, and pull them apart at one of the short ends. Carefully lay them flat, glue side up, and do not disturb until they have dried overnight. Brush on a thin coat of India ink. When thoroughly dry, sand lightly with very fine sandpaper until the vein design appears.

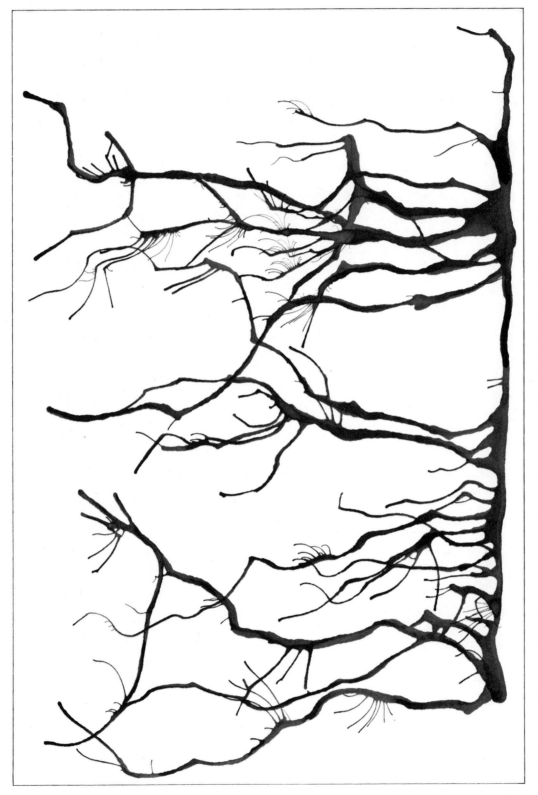

21. Using a small brush, make an ink line across the bottom of a panel, applying the ink heavily so the ink line remains very wet, as in a puddle. Using an air brush with 25 lbs. pressure but no ink in the cup, blow air "upward" from the bottom of the panel towards the top, holding the air brush at an angle of about 30° with the surface. Tree-like shapes will sprout from the ink-line puddle and "grow" upward.

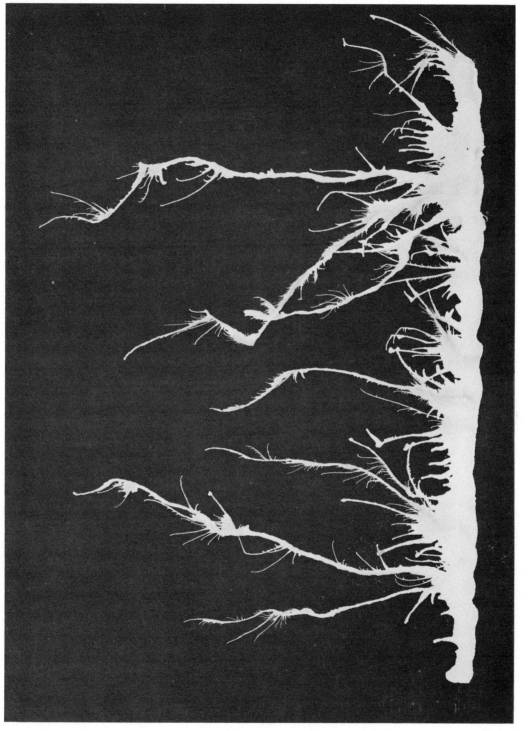

22. Proceed as for Design 21, but use Johnston's Special Grade White ink in place of India ink, on a black panel.

Fig. 17.

Fig. 19.

Fig. 16.

Fig. 18.

Fig. 21.

Fig. 20.

cracks
and crackle

Layers in Tension

The ceramist may work carefully to produce cracks and crackle in his pottery because he knows that this adds aesthetic appeal. Part of the charm of old paintings is due to the natural aging process which darkens and subdues the colors and covers the canvas with a fine network of cracks and crackle. Albert Pinkham Ryder's paintings are remembered for their mysterious romantic quality, most due to his skill and intuitive talent, but partly due to accident—the artist's poor judgment in the use of paints, varnishes, and driers in ways that made them crack and crackle at a very early age. Who can visualize the works of Ryder without the fissures that are as much a part of the picture as the subject matter itself? ■ The painting contractor or the do-it-yourselfer may work hard to coat a surface with a smooth, even layer of paint without blemishes of any kind. It isn't easy because differences in hardness of paint layers cause *checking*. The sliding of one paint layer over another results in the fissures known as *alligatoring*. *Cracking* and *scaling* are due to brittleness of the paint film. ■ The shapes and forms occurring in layers of materials under stress are evident in nature in many places besides paint film. Crackle on the surface of a delicate piece of pottery is caused by contraction of the glaze. On an asphalt street, the constantly changing temperature, the layers of material beneath the surface, and the pounding of the traffic cause cracks. The bark of some trees has a pattern of cracks and ridges formed by the stretching of the growing tree's outer coat. The muddy soil at the edge of a pond dries and contracts as the sun's heat removes the moisture, forming a network of cracks. ■ Shapes and forms resulting from layers under stress are our concern in this chapter.

Fig. 16: Cracks in dried mud. □ **Fig. 17:** Cracks in thin ice surface. □ **Fig. 18:** Crackle on surface of ceramic bowl. □ **Fig. 19:** Broken glass. □ **Fig. 20:** Cracks in asphalt street. **Fig. 21:** Tree bark. Photos for Figs. 16, 17, 19, 20 and 21 by author.

31

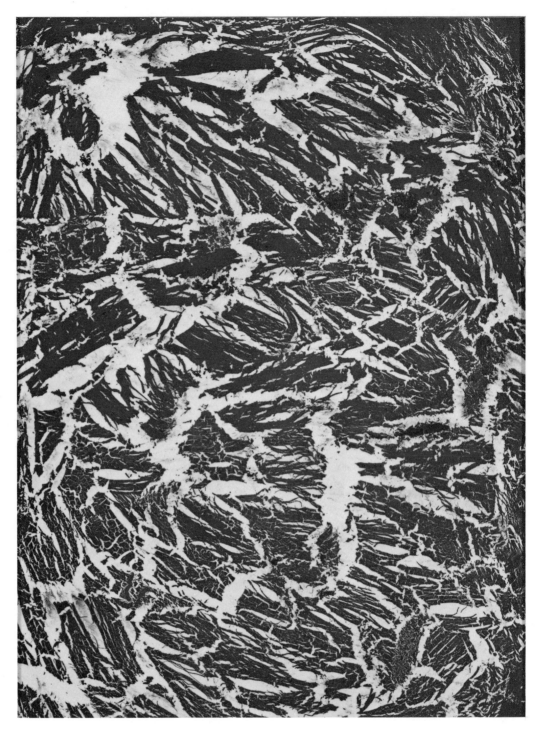

23. Coat a piece of illustration board with Elmer's Glue-All, making the brush strokes at random in different directions. While the glue is still wet, apply a coat of India ink, again applying the ink in strokes in different directions. Allow to dry.

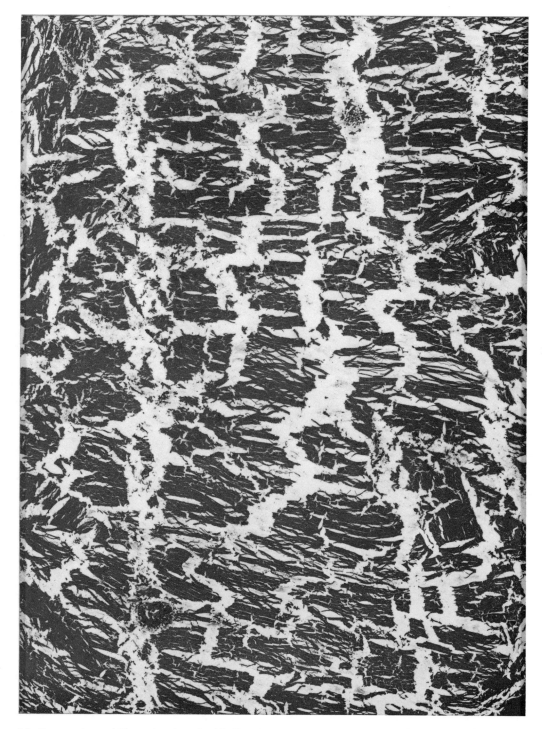

24. Coat a piece of illustration board with Elmer's Glue-All, making the brush strokes lengthwise along the panel. While the glue is still wet, flow on a coat of Higgins India ink, making the brush strokes crosswise on the panel (at right angles to the glue brush strokes). Use a soft sable brush, preferably about ½"; be sure to wash it out quickly with water after using, as the ink tends to harden and damage the bristles.

25. Enlargement of part of Design 24.

26. Enlargement of part of Color Plate C (following page 88).

27. Coat a piece of illustration board with Elmer's Glue-All, brushing it on the panel in concentric circles. While the glue is still wet, brush on orange Pelikan Drawing Ink, following roughly the same pattern of brush strokes that was established by the glue brush strokes.

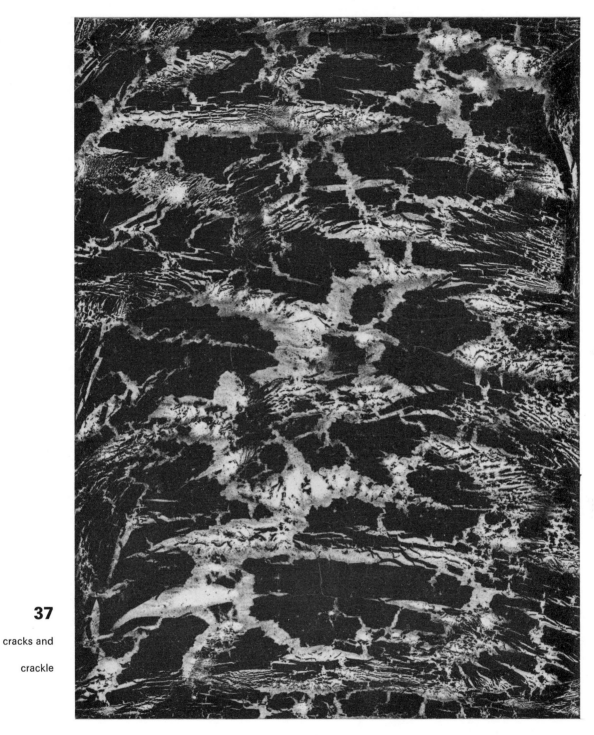

28. Apply a coating of LePage's Glue to the surface, in a fairly thick coat. Immediately brush on a coat of black poster color. As they dry, the pattern appears. When this is completely dry, brush on a coat of clear lacquer, or spray with Krylon, as the glue tends to become sticky if the weather is damp, and should be isolated from the atmosphere.

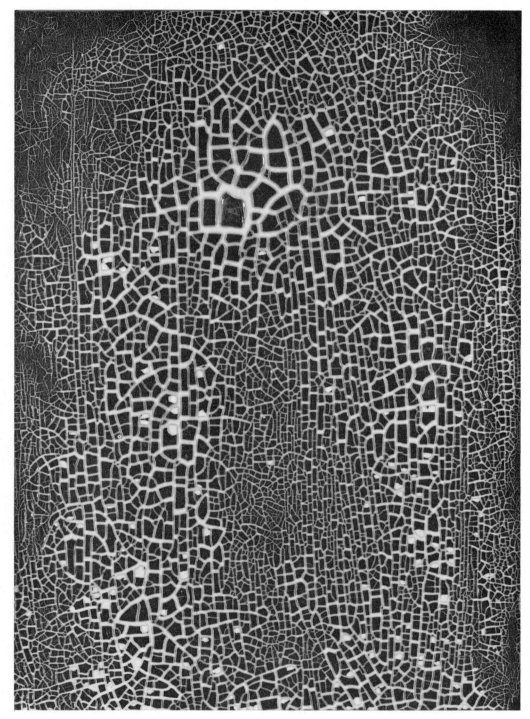

29. A coat of Higgins White Paste is applied to the illustration board, about ⅛″ thick. A coat of India ink is flowed on with a soft brush, while the paste is still wet. This particular effect requires quite a long drying time, at least overnight. When completely dry, there is danger that the little raised pieces of dried ink will loosen and fall off, so it is a good idea to apply a thick coat of lacquer with a soft brush. If any of the design does loosen during the process, push the pieces in place with a needle or pin, and the lacquer will hold them in place when it dries.

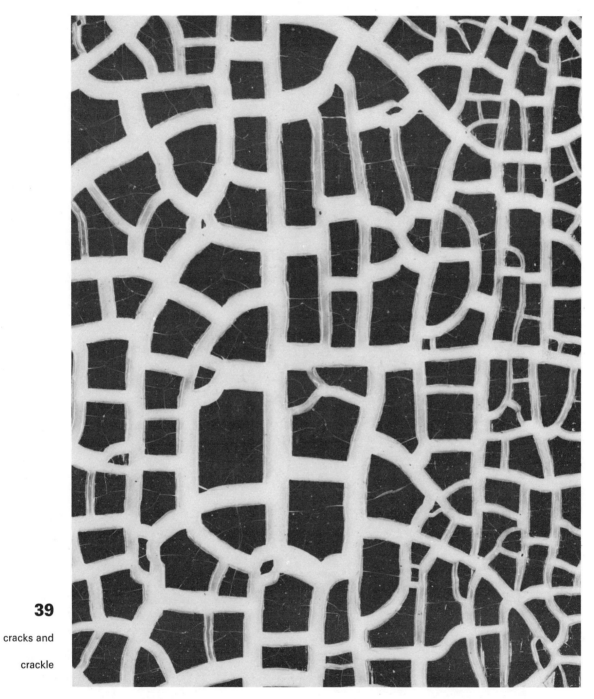

30. Enlargement of part of Design 29.

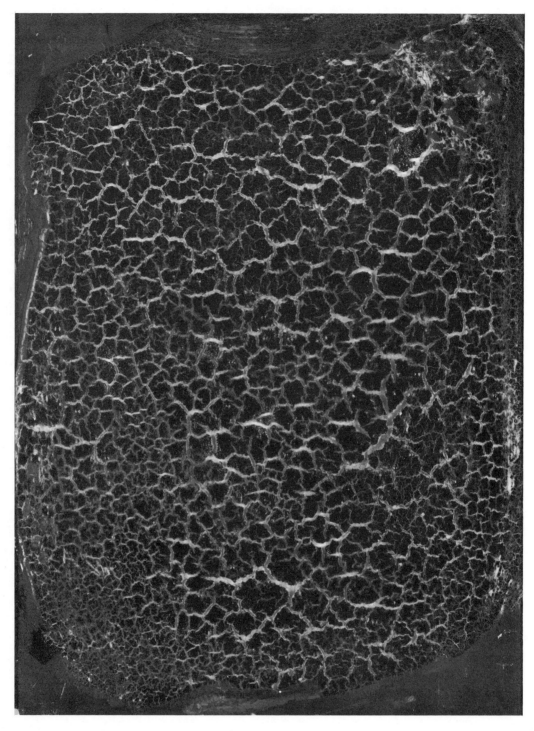

31. Make a thick flour paste, simply by mixing flour and water. Apply to illustration board in a coat about ⅛" thick. Flow on a coat of India ink with a soft brush while the paste is still wet. Allow to dry for a full day. After the cracks have formed and the material is completely dry, flow on a thick coat of lacquer with a soft brush, to keep pieces from chipping off.

32. Coat illustration board that has been sprayed with black enamel with LePage's liquid brown glue. While still wet, apply a coat of white poster color, and allow to dry.

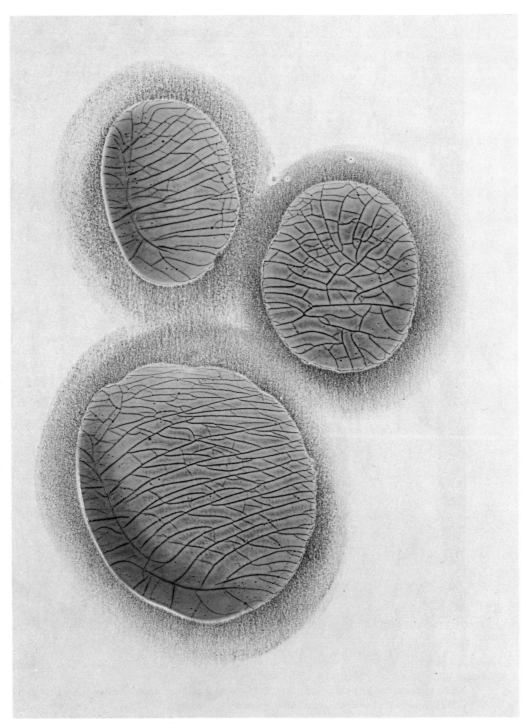

33. Using a brush, make several large blobs of LePage's Glue on the surface of a panel, and allow to dry overnight flat on a table. When it is completely dry, rub a little black powdered pigment (Grumbacher's) over the surface with the forefinger. The pigment catches in the cracks and crevices, revealing a pattern. Spray with fixative.

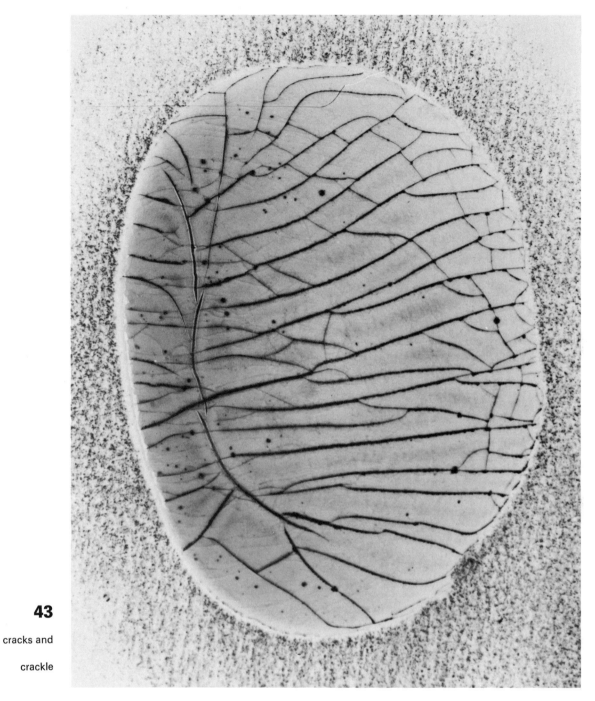

34. Enlargement of part of Design 33.

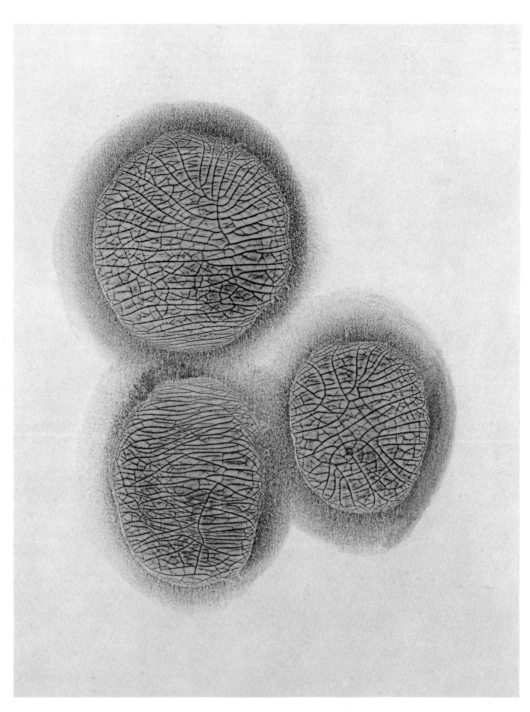

35. Follow the same procedure as for Design 33, but use Carter's Liquid Paste instead of LePage's Glue.

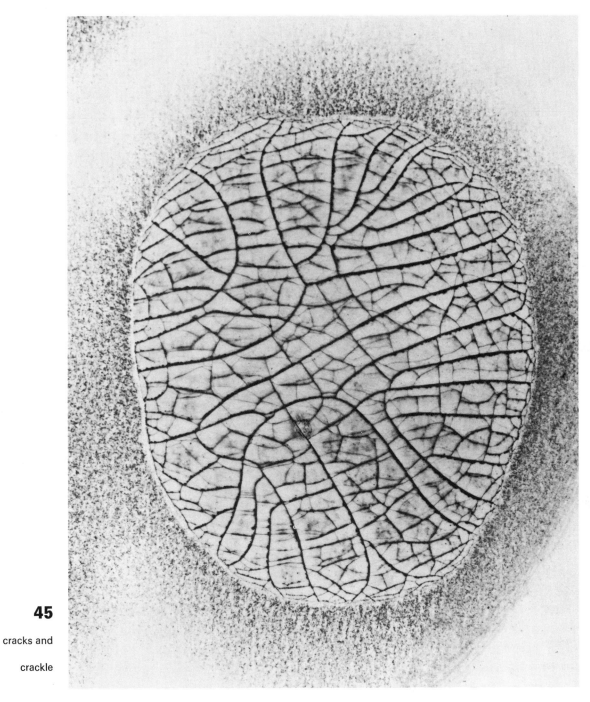

36. Enlargement of part of Design 35.

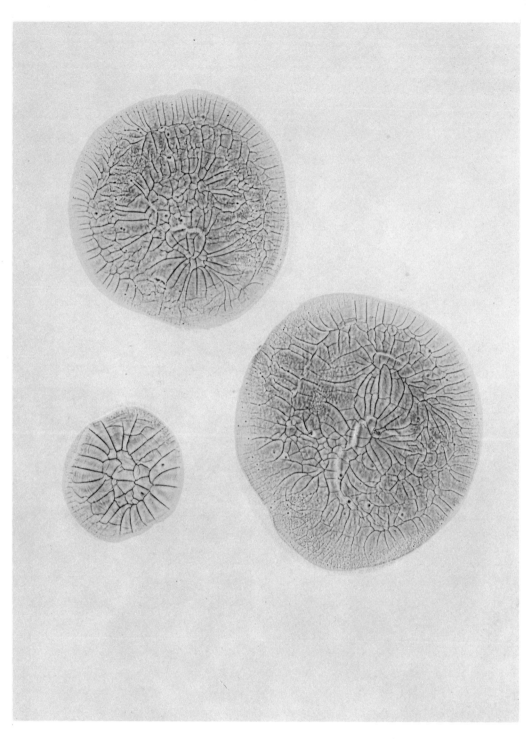

37. Follow the same procedure as for Design 33, but use white showcard color (Crown Tempera Color) instead of LePage's Glue.

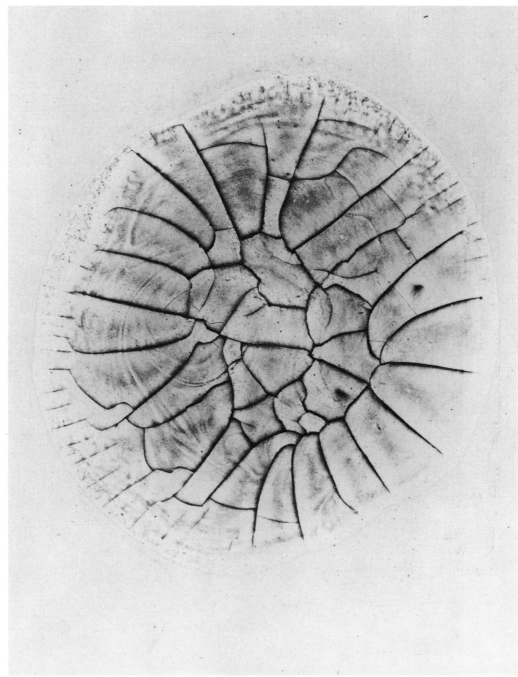

38. Enlargement of part of Design 37.

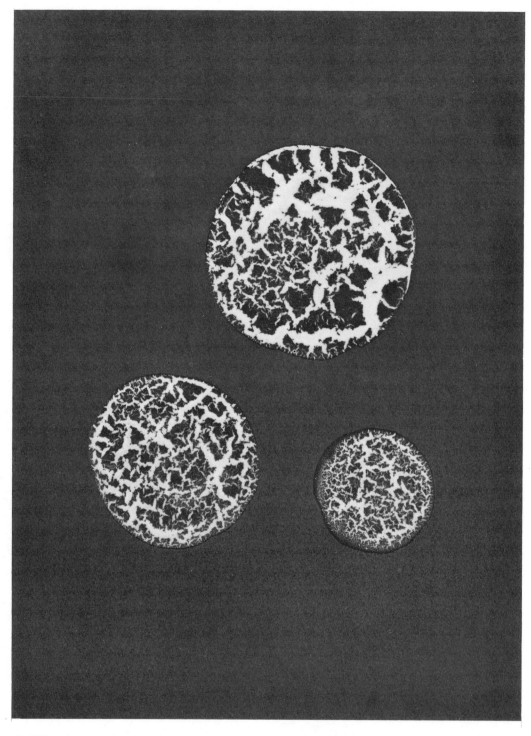

39. Using a brush, make several large blobs of Elmer's Glue-All on the surface of a panel. Immediately spray with black India ink while the glue is still wet. Allow to dry overnight.

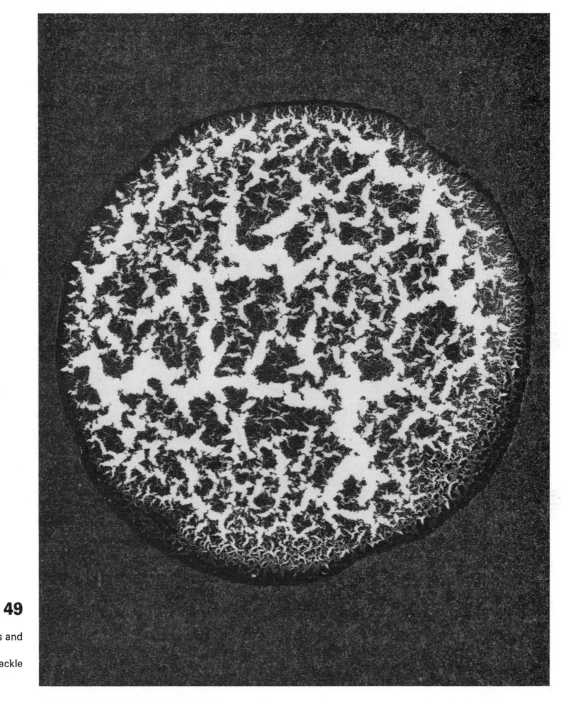

40. Enlargement of part of Design 39.

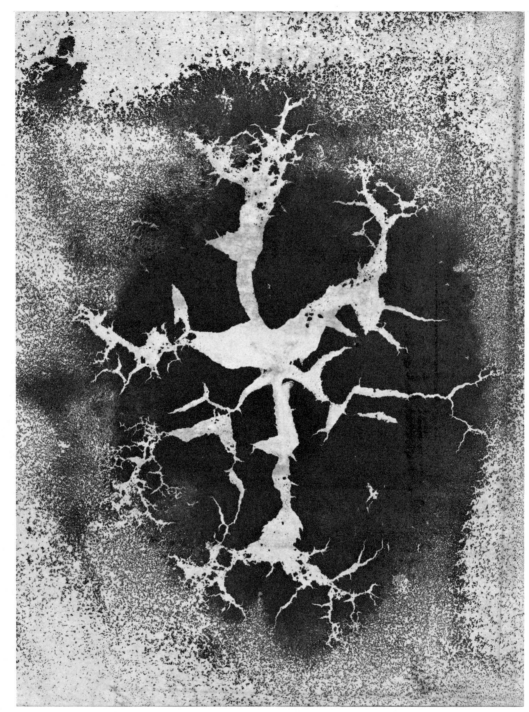

41. Hold a piece of illustration board under water until it is thoroughly soaked. Pick up the panel by the tip of one corner and allow the water to drain off until it has stopped running off in a steady stream, and is falling off in drops. Quickly place it on an old newspaper, flat on a table. Drop a small quantity of graphite, about the size of a pea, in the center of the panel, and blow downward on it, causing it to spread over the surface of the panel. Take a toothpick or match that has been dipped into liquid detergent, and touch it to the center of the graphite area. A broad radiating crack will appear in the graphite. Allow it to dry for about an hour without disturbing, and then spray with fixative. After a few hours, spray again.

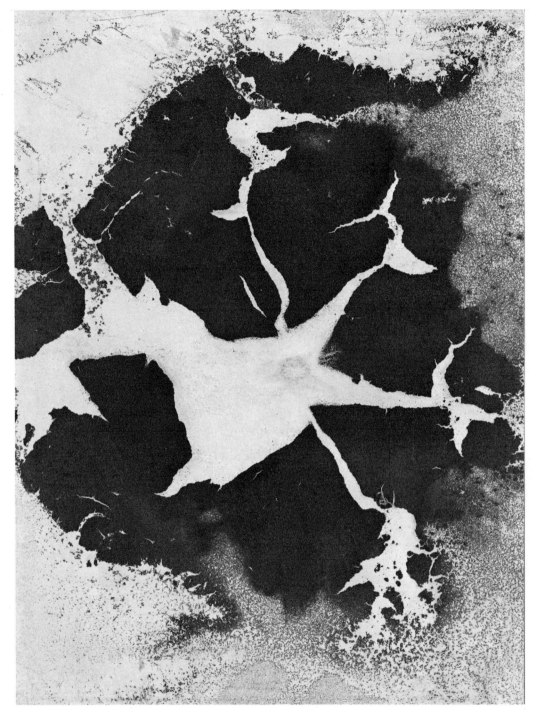

42. Variation of Design 41.

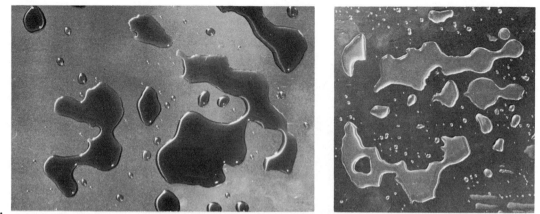

Fig. 22 .

Fig. 26 .

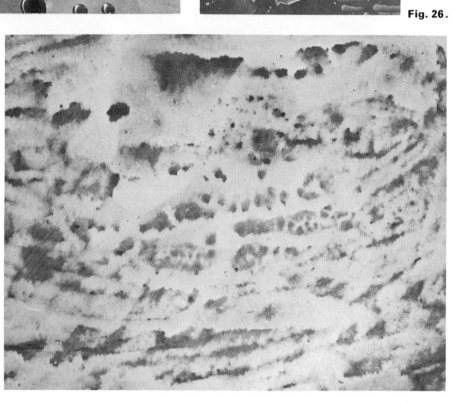

Fig. 23 .

Fig. 24 .

Fig. 25 .

crawl Rejection of Paint

by an Incompatible Surface

When rain falls on the smooth and highly polished surface of an automobile it seems to draw itself away from the waxy surface. ■ Anyone who has used paint for home repair jobs can probably recall an occasion when paint was applied to some unsuitable surface. Instead of adhering properly, the paint drew up into small puddles, or else left a thin coat in some areas and created undesirable irregular shapes of thicker pigment in scattered places. Usually the cause of this *crawling* is the application of paint to a surface which is very smooth and lacks enough tooth for the paint to take hold. A water-base paint will be rejected by a surface that has an oily character—just as oily paint is rejected when applied to a surface that is damp with water. ■ When a wave breaks on the edge of the seashore, the layer of foam that is created quickly dissipates, forming momentary patterns that are very much like crawling paint, the great difference being that the foam vanishes completely and rapidly, while crawling paint retains its design on the surface. In a similar but slower process, a layer of melting snow on an open field forms characteristic irregular patterns as the snow melts and "withdraws." ■ Some of the designs in this chapter are the result of rejection of paint by very smooth surfaces. Others resulted when a pigment was applied over a still-wet coat of incompatible paint or glue and the layers reacted, forming their own typical pattern.

Fig. 22: Water on glass. □ **Fig. 23:** Sea foam on water at edge of beach. □ **Fig. 24:** White water-base paint applied to smooth shellac surface. □ **Fig. 25:** Melting snow in field. **Fig. 26:** Water on polished metal surface. Photos by author.

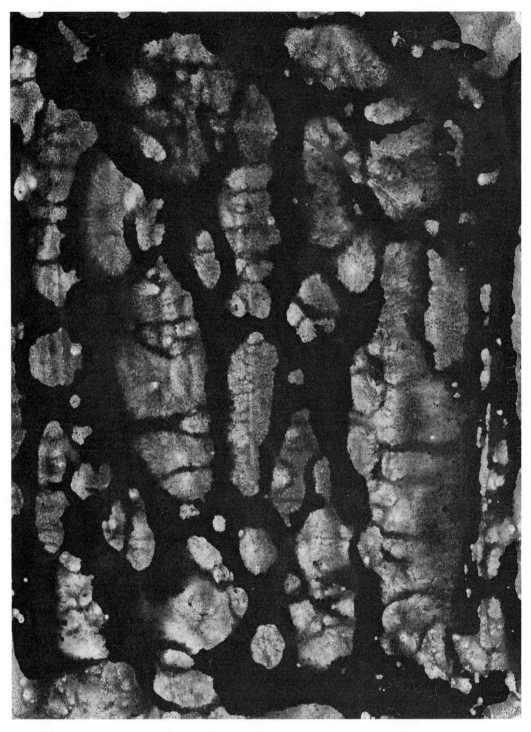

43. Coat illustration board with white shellac. After drying for 15 minutes, quickly apply a coat of India ink with a ½″ brush. Allow to dry.

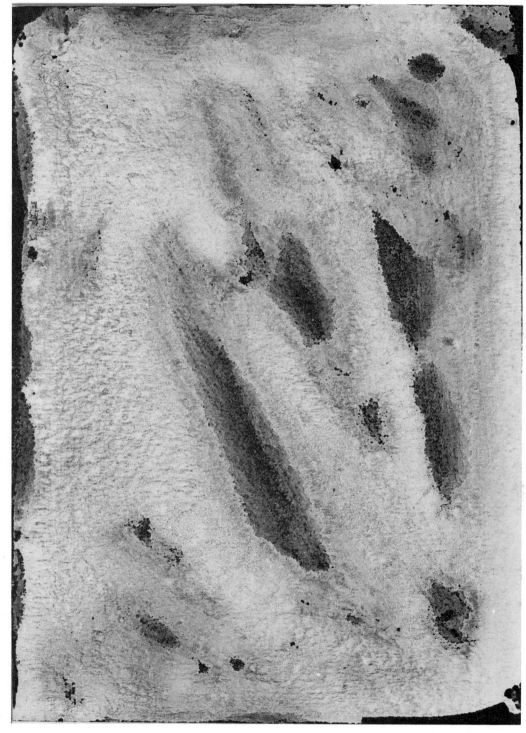

44. Black paper is coated with white shellac and allowed to dry. If necessary, an additional coat of shellac is given to make the paper waterproof. Allow to dry. With a large brush, flow on a coat of white showcard color mixed with water (1 part paint to 2 parts water). Allow to dry and spray with fixative.

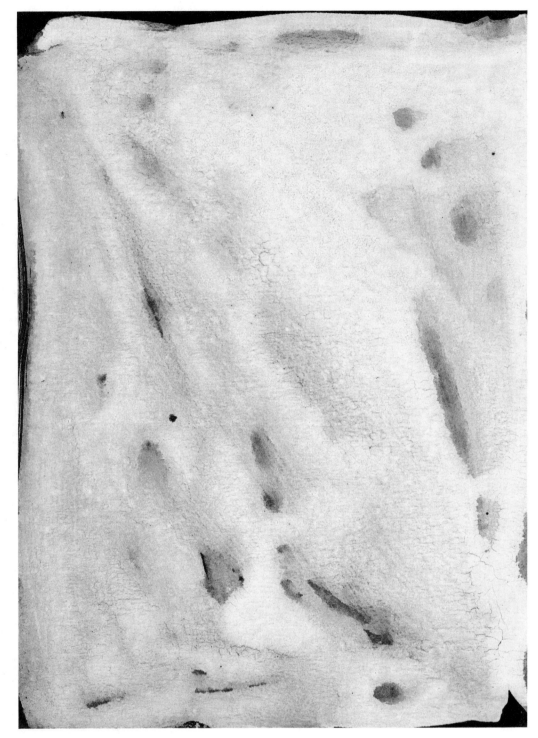

56

crawl

45. Variation of Design 44.

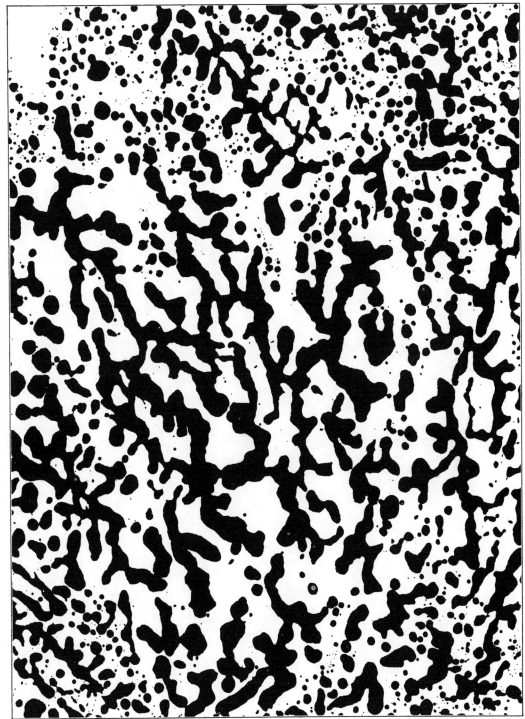

46. A coat of black showcard color is painted onto the surface of a sheet of thin, transparent plastic of the type sometimes used by laundries to protect clean clothing. The plastic rejects the paint, which forms small, irregular puddles. Quickly place the plastic sheet, painted surface down, on a sheet of absorbent white paper (in this case, it was newsprint). The design is transferred.

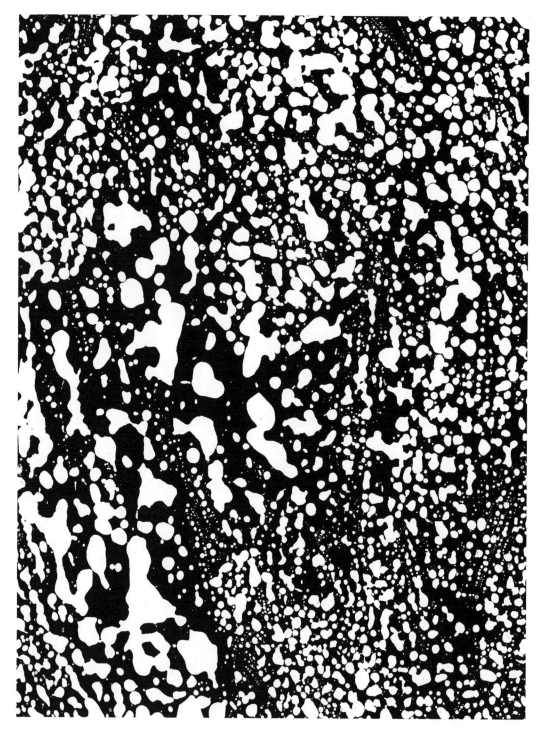

47. Follow the same procedure as for Design 46, using white paint and transferring the design onto black paper.

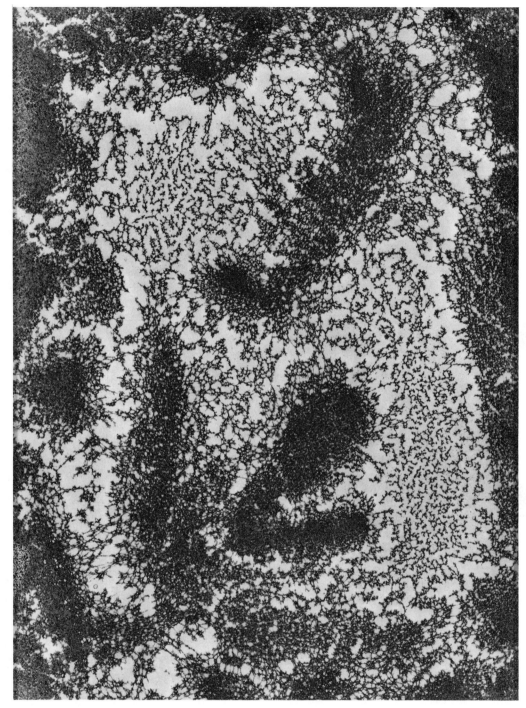

48. Apply a thick coat of white shellac to an illustration board panel that is laid flat on a table. Quickly spray on a coat of black lacquer, before the shellac has a chance to dry. As the lacquer dries, it contracts, forming a fine-veined plant-like pattern. Where the lacquer is thickest, the veins stand out most clearly.

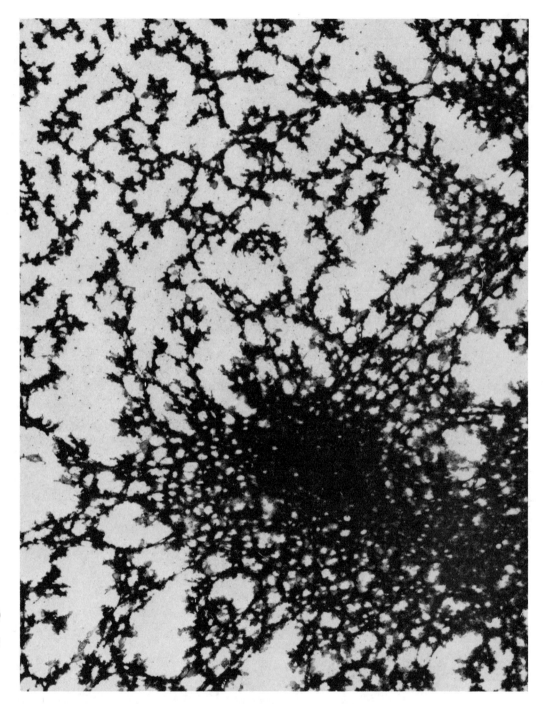

49. Enlargement of part of Design 48.

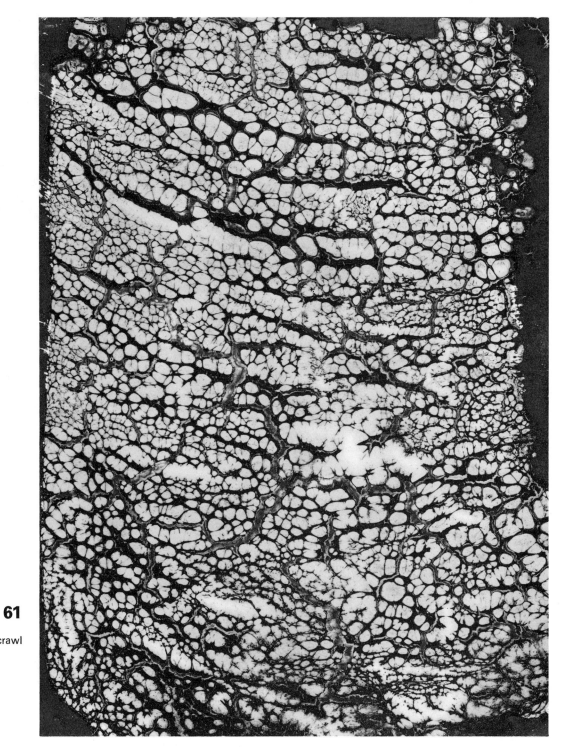

50. Cover the surface with a thick coat of Duco Household Cement. While it is still wet, quickly apply a coat of black showcard color. Allow to dry for several hours.

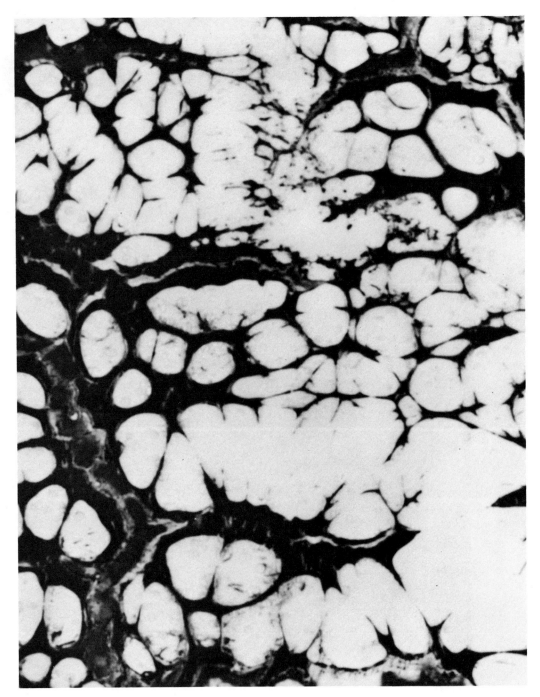

51. Enlargement of part of Design 50.

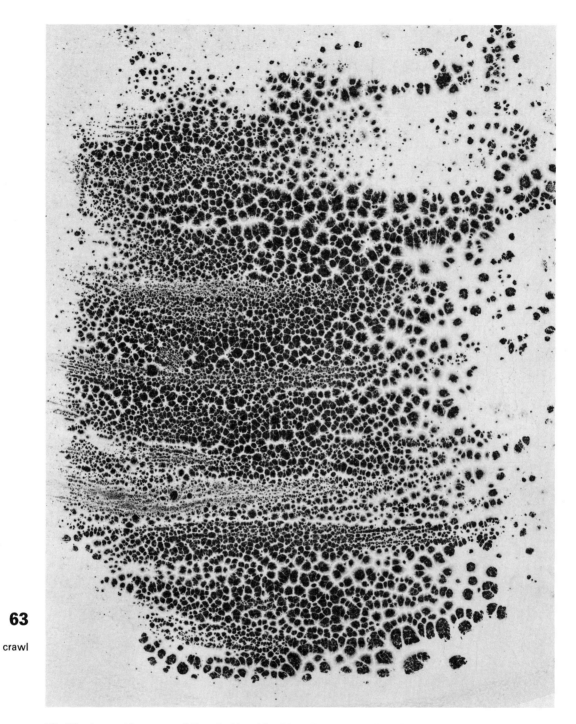

63

crawl

52. Mix three tablespoons of Elmer's Glue-All with enough Grumbacher's black powdered pigment to make the glue completely black. Smear it thickly over the surface of the illustration board and coat with white showcard color while it is still wet. Allow to dry for a couple of hours.

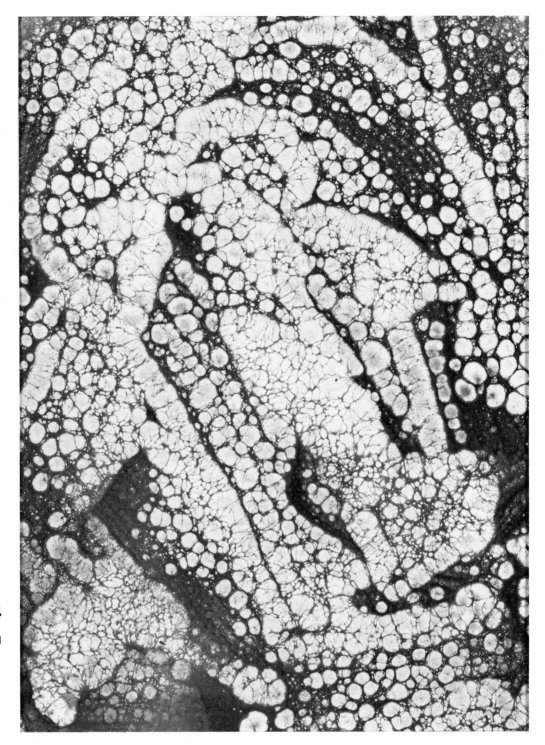

53. A thick coat of white showcard color is slopped onto the surface of a piece of illustration board with a 1″ brush. Immediately, black India ink is sprayed onto the surface.

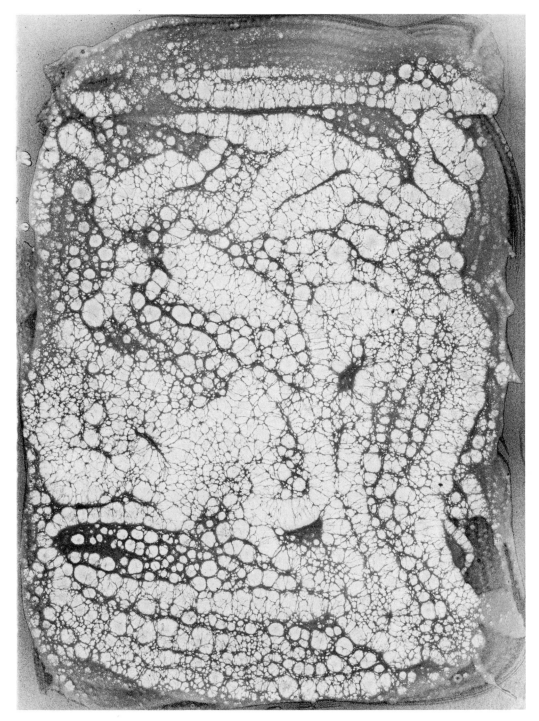

54. Variation of Design 53.

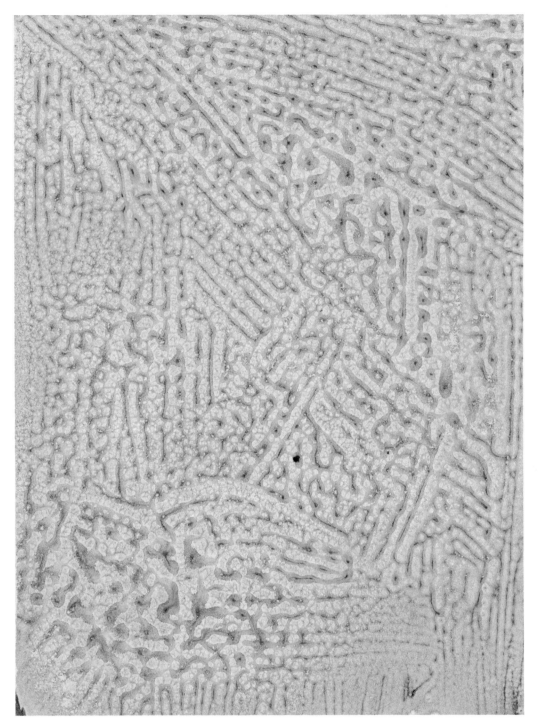

55. A thick coat of white showcard color is brushed onto the surface. About 20 drops of liquid detergent (Vel was used on this one) are dropped onto the surface and thoroughly mixed with the paint. India ink is immediately sprayed over the still-wet surface with an air brush.

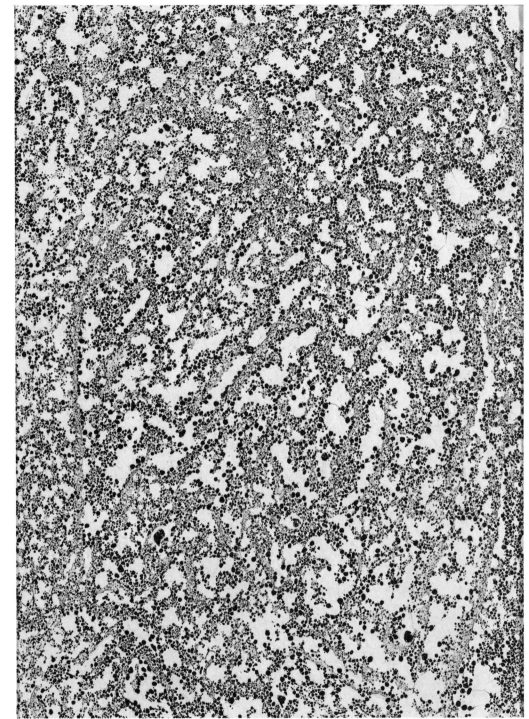

56. Cover the surface of the panel with a thick coat of Miracle Black adhesive, using a palette knife. While it is still wet, brush on a coat of white showcard color. Allow to dry.

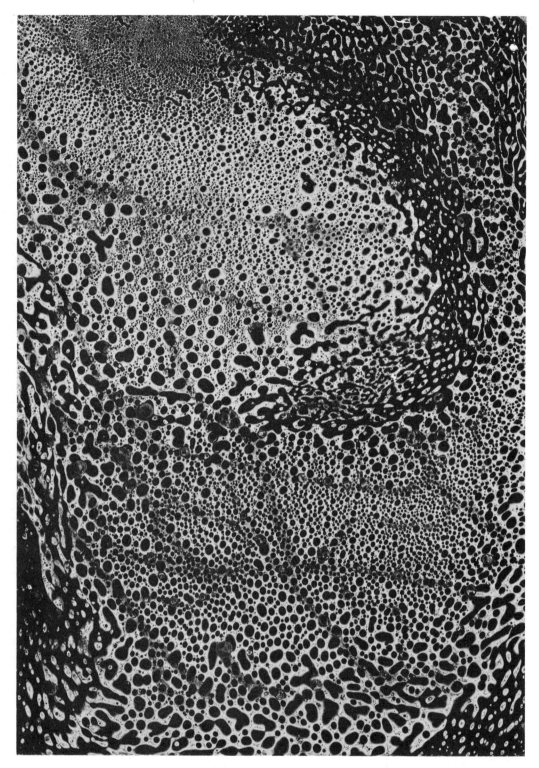

68

crawl

57. Pour water into a baking pan until it is about ¾ full. The pan used to make this illustration measured 9″ × 12″ × 2″ deep. Using black enamel in a spray container, spray the surface of the water heavily until globules of enamel form on the surface. Hold a cardboard panel by the edges and quickly lower it into the water, face downward. Tilt the panel at a slight angle while lowering it into the water, to prevent air from being trapped by panel. Remove quickly and place on a piece of newspaper until dry.

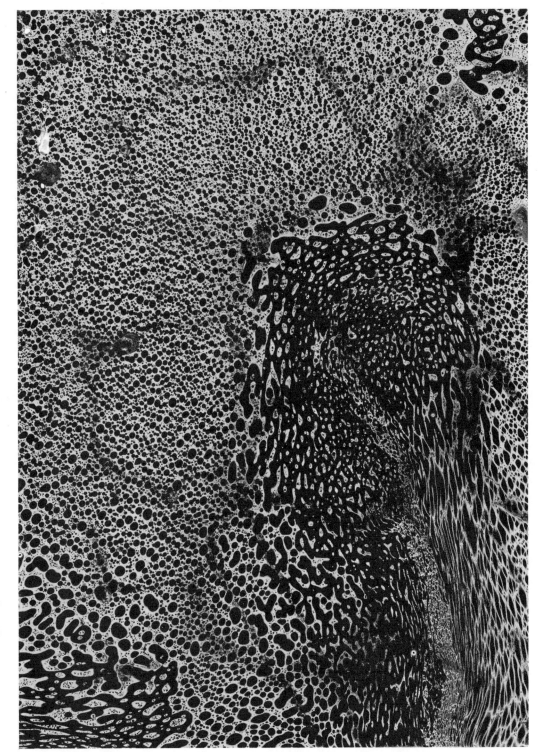

58. Variation of Design 57.

Fig. 27.

Fig. 28.

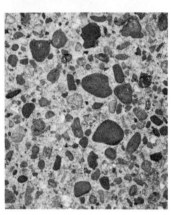

Fig. 32.

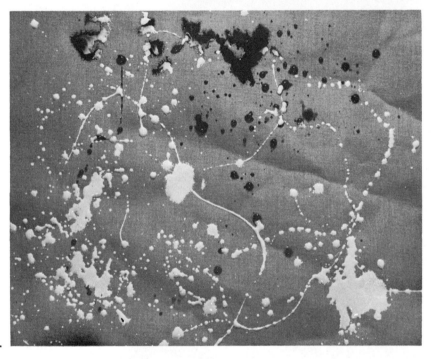

Fig. 29.

Fig. 30.

Fig. 31.

drip, dribble, drop

Pollock's Discovery and Random Patterns

The canvas drop-cloth used by a painting contractor to protect furniture and floors gradually develops a wide collection of accidental drips and dribbles in a variety of colors. It took Jackson Pollock to recognize the visual appeal of the random dropping of paint, and to declare that dribbled paint could be appropriate subject matter for a work of art. Designs made by the "drip-and-dribble" method are easy to make, and watching the endless variety of forms and shapes materialize is an experience with almost hypnotic fascination. If the paint is very viscous, the dribbles are almost like string, and form intricate graceful curves on a canvas or panel. ■ The random dropping of paint onto a surface has its counterpart in the random dropping of colored pieces of paper or other material onto a panel and gluing them in place where they fall. In nature, this effect is most obviously seen in the patterns made by fallen leaves on the ground, or by a handful of cigarettes or playing cards tossed onto a table— and at the seashore, where the ocean has thrown a collection of pebbles or shells onto the sandy beach. ■ A "controlled" use of random arrangements is made in terrazzo flooring. An assortment of marble chips in cement is poured onto a flat surface and after hardening is polished smooth, revealing the accidental relationships of the small pieces of marble. A similar effect is used in the design of some types of plastic tile, and in table or floor coverings.

Fig. 27: Dropped string. □ **Fig. 28:** Playing cards tossed onto table. □ **Fig. 29:** House painter's drop-cloth. □ **Fig. 30:** Random arrangement of cigarettes. □ **Fig. 31:** Terrazzo. **Fig. 32:** Pebbles on beach. Photos for Figs. 27 through 30 and Fig. 32 by author.

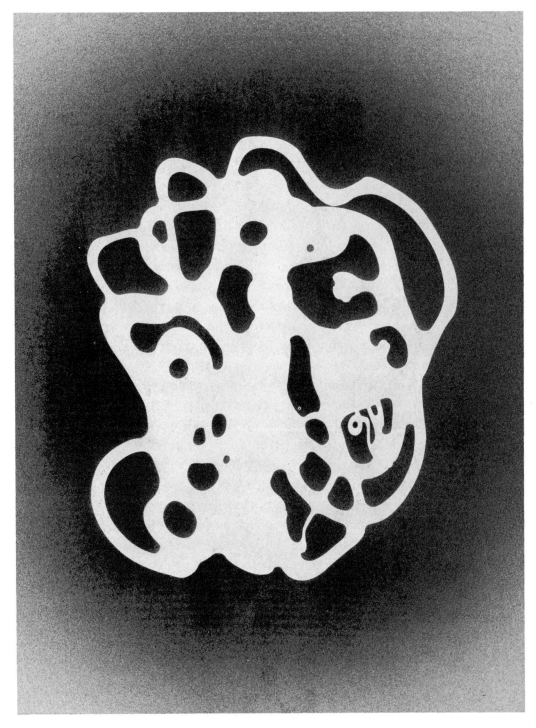

59. Dribble rubber cement (Best-Test) from its container over the surface of the panel, keeping it away from the edges. Allow to set for about 10 minutes, leaving the panel flat. Spray on a coat of black watercolor paint or air brush retouching color. After the black paint has dried for about 10 minutes, gently lay a sheet of scrap paper on the panel, then carefully lift it off—it will remove a layer of rubber cement with it. Repeat this process several times until almost all the rubber cement has been removed. With the fingers, remove surplus by rubbing. During the whole operation try to avoid smearing the paint and cement.

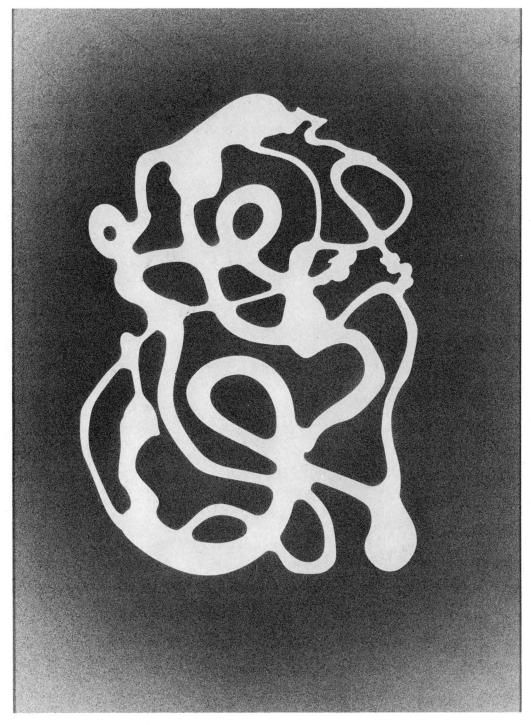

73

drip, dribble,

drop

60. Variation of Design 59.

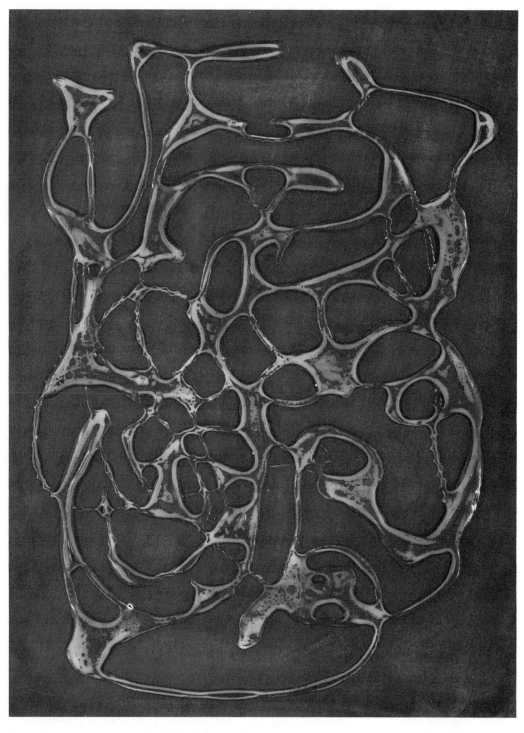

61. Dribble a stream of Elmer's Glue-All from a plastic squeeze-bottle onto the surface of the panel. Allow to dry overnight. Brush on a coat of India ink. After it is thoroughly dry, rub the surface lightly with a damp cloth until some of the ink is removed.

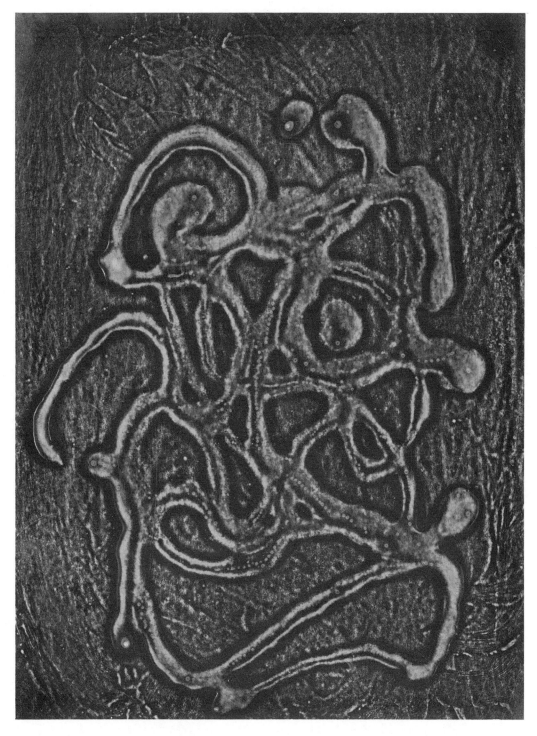

62. Spread a thin coat of Elmer's Glue-All onto the surface of the panel with the fingers and lay panel **flat.** Dribble a stream of the same glue from a plastic squeeze-bottle over the surface and allow to dry overnight. Brush on a coat of India ink. After thorough drying, sand lightly with very fine sandpaper.

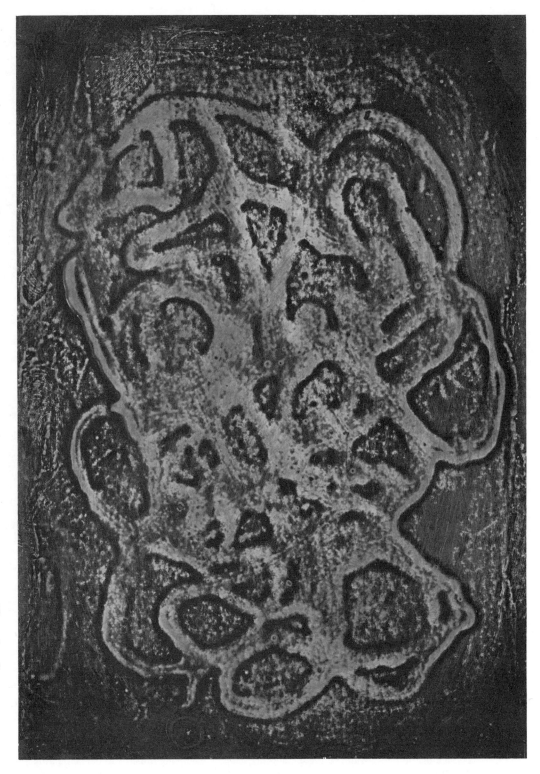

76

drip, dribble,

drop

63. Variation of Design 62.

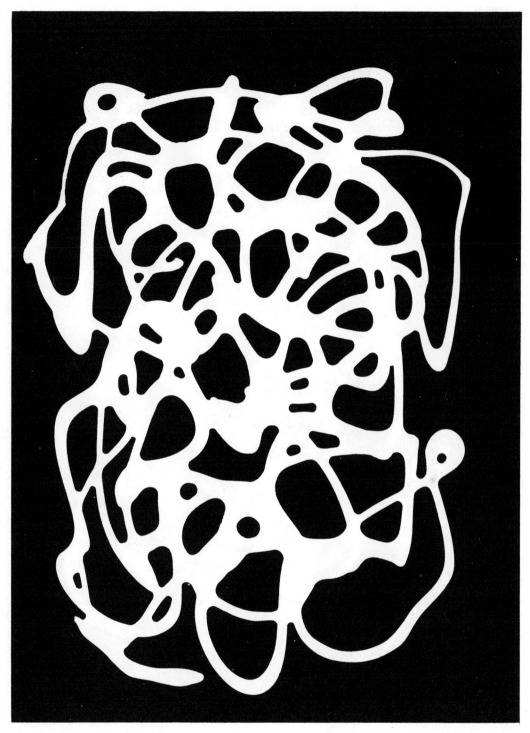

64. Rubber cement is poured into a plastic squeeze-bottle container (the type that has a pointed screw-on top, and is sometimes used by women for applying hair-wave preparations or hair dye). The bottle is held about two feet above a panel laid flat on a table, and rubber cement is dribbled over the surface. The panel is then set aside to dry; an hour is about long enough. The surface of the panel is then sprayed with ink or watercolor, using an air brush. After the surface is dry, lightly press a sheet of newspaper onto the surface to remove any damp ink from the rubber cement. Rub the surface of the rubber cement lightly with the fingers in order to remove it and reveal the design.

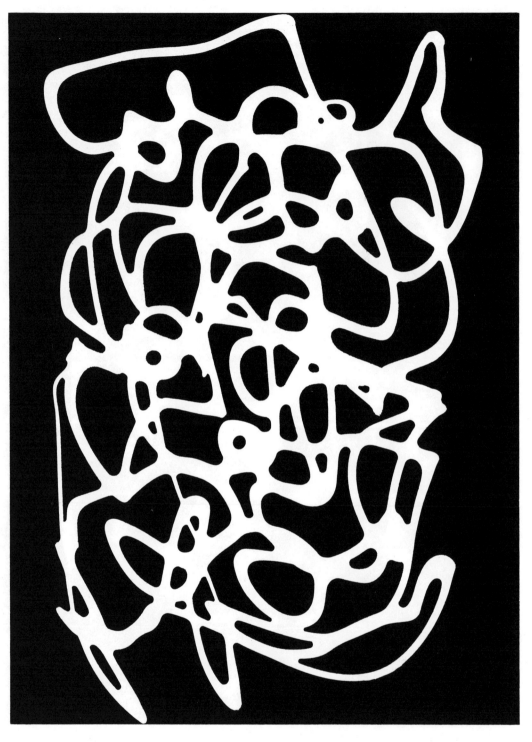

78

drip, dribble,

drop

65. Variation of Design 64.

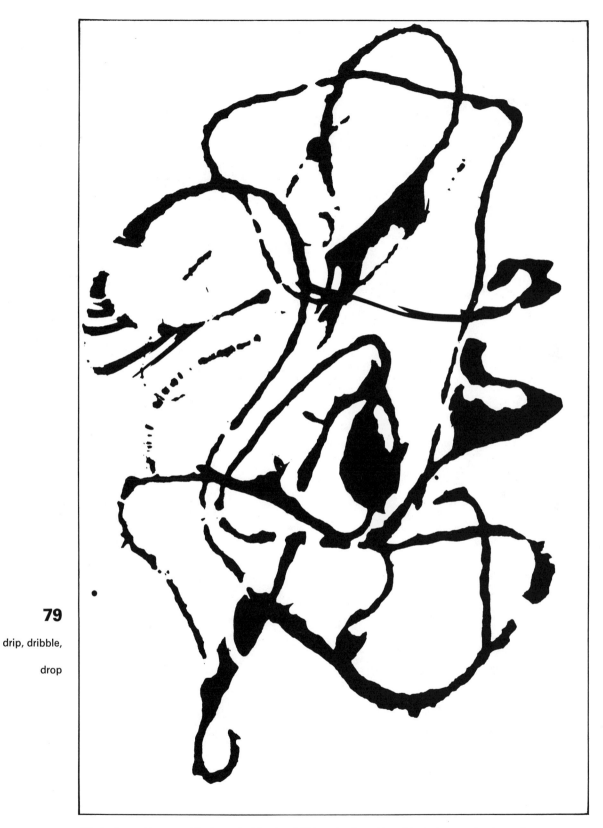

79

drip, dribble,

drop

66. A piece of heavy white household string 18″ long is dipped into black showcard color and then lowered onto a white panel twice.

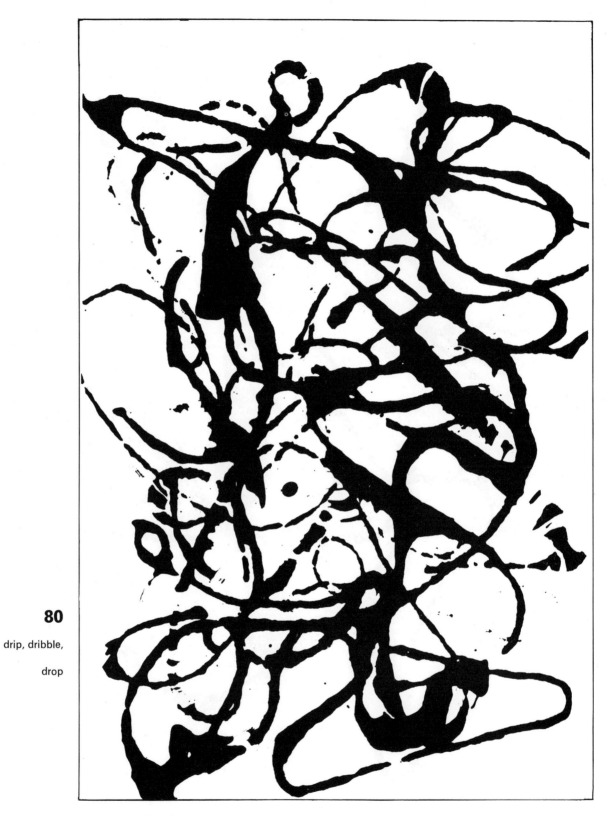

67. Proceed as for Design 66, but lower the string five times, dipping it in showcard color each time.

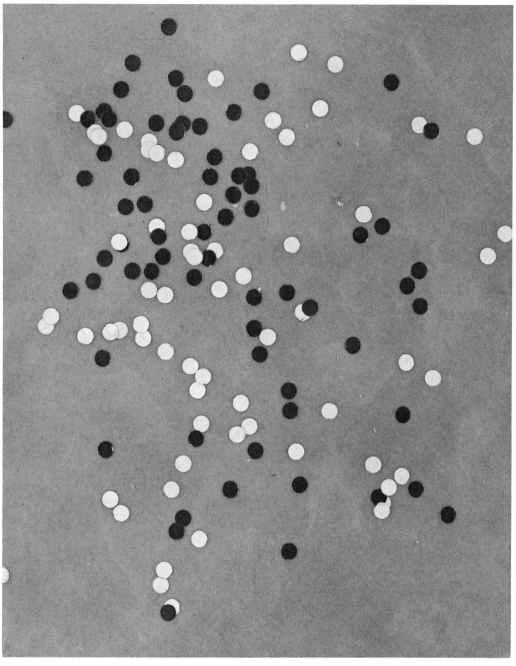

68. Use a standard 2- or 3-hole paper punch that makes ¼" holes, and punch holes in black Color-Vu paper until 100 or 150 punched pieces have accumulated. (Color-Vu paper is colored on one side and white on the other). Smear a thick coat of Elmer's Glue-All over the surface of a medium grey panel, using the fingers. Sprinkle punched paper on the surface from a height of 2 or 3 feet, in a random pattern. After this is thoroughly dry, smear on another coat of glue to secure the pieces of paper.

69. Cut black Color-Vu paper into odd scraps until 75 or 100 pieces have accumulated. Proceed as in Design 68.

83

drip, dribble,

drop

70. Cut pieces of heavy white paper into 20 uniform strips, ¼" × 3". Coat a black panel with Elmer's Glue-All, spreading it with the fingers. Drop the strips one at a time from a height of 2 or 3 feet. When the moisture of the glue makes the ends of the paper curl upward, lightly press down the tips with a pencil until they hold in place. After they are thoroughly dry, they can again be coated with glue to make sure they are securely held in place.

71. Proceed as for Design 70, but use black paper on a white background.

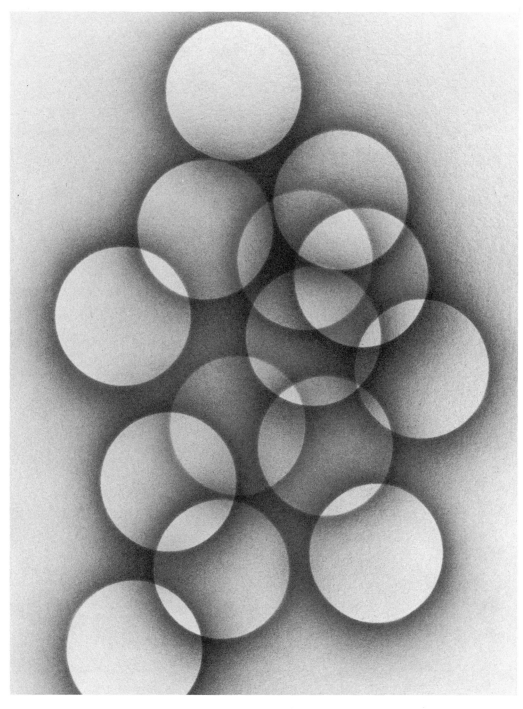

72. Carefully cut out a cardboard circle 2 inches in diameter. Drop it from a height of 2 feet onto a panel laid flat on a table. Hold the circle in position with a small weight and spray around the edges, using an air brush and black watercolor. Repeat operation 14 times.

86

drip, dribble,

drop

73. Proceed as for Design 72, but use a square with a 1½″ side.

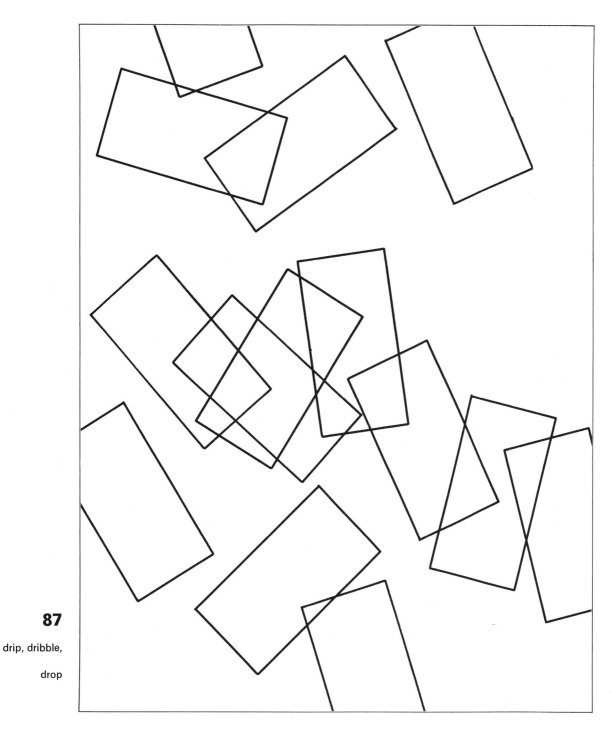

74. Cut out a cardboard rectangle 1¼" × 2½". Drop it from a height of about 2 feet onto a panel laid flat on a table. Outline the rectangle where it falls. Repeat the operation 14 times. The outlines in this illustration were made with a No. 3 Leroy pen held in a Leroy penholder, using India ink.

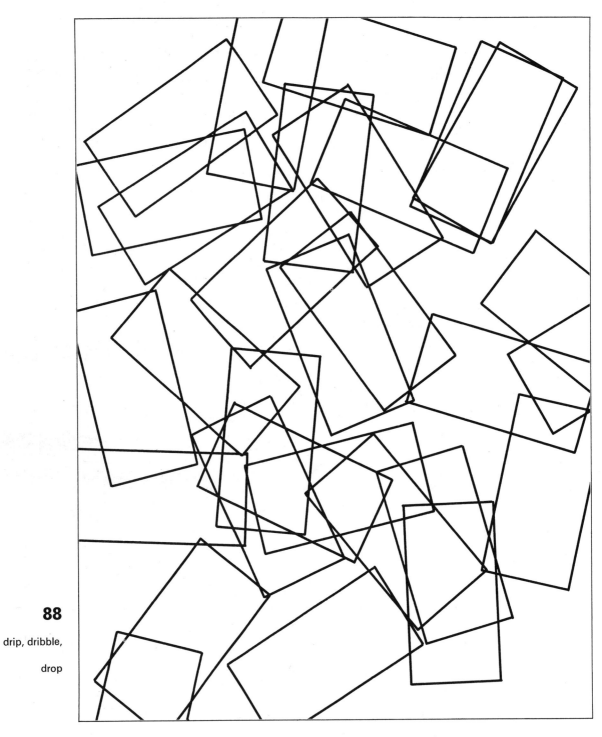

75. Variation of Design 74 in which the rectangle is dropped 30 times.

A. (Tree Forms.) Use Crayola crayons. Rub the surface of the illustration board with yellow crayon until it is completely covered. Take several crayons: red, red-orange, orange, yellow-orange; remove the paper wrapping and scrape each crayon with a sharp knife, allowing the shavings to fall on the surface of the illustration board at random. With the panel lying flat, hold an electric heat lamp close enough to the surface of the panel to allow the wax to melt. Some judgment should be used to prevent the wax from catching on fire. Move the lamp slowly over the surface in order to cover the whole area, and keep as much of it as possible heated, until the colors fuse.

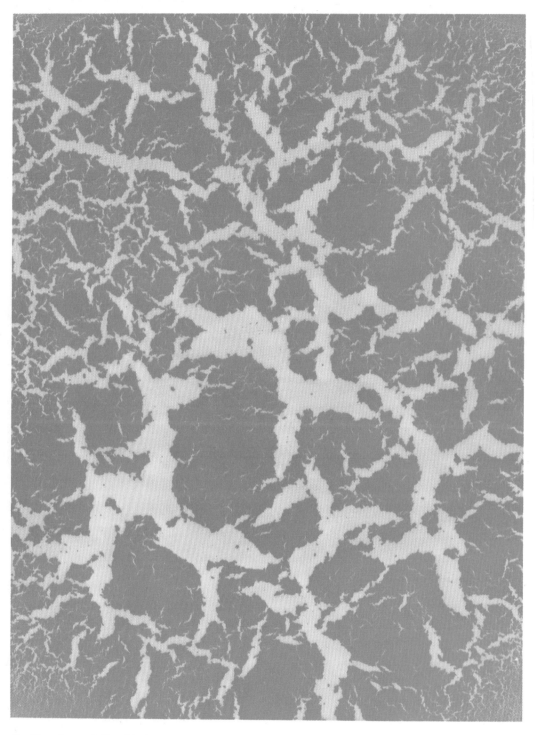

B. (Cracks and Crackle.) Apply a thick coat of Elmer's Glue-All to the surface of a piece of illustration board. While it is still wet, spray on a coat of green Pelikan Drawing Ink, covering the surface as quickly as possible. Allow to lie flat until dry.

C. (Cracks and Crackle.) Coat a piece of illustration board with Elmer's Glue-All, making the brush strokes lengthwise along the panel. While the glue is still wet, flow on a coat of Pelikan Red Drawing Ink, making the brush strokes lengthwise, in the same direction as the glue strokes. Allow to dry.

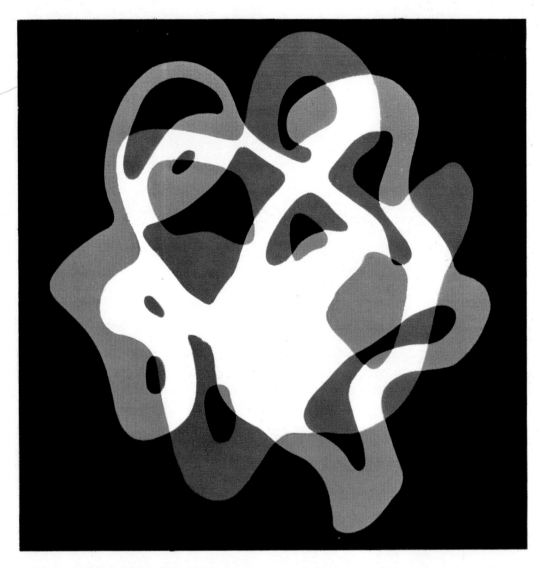

D. (Drip, Dribble, Drop.) This design was produced with rubber cement and colored inks. As in the preparation of Design 59 (page 72), the rubber cement was applied to a white panel. Red ink was sprayed on; then the cement was removed. A different application of rubber cement was made, then green ink was sprayed on. Where the rubber cement areas overlapped, there are white areas; where ink areas overlapped, there are brown areas; the rest is red and green.

E. (Drip, Dribble, Drop.) Dribble a small amount of rubber cement onto the surface of the illustration board. After it has set for about 10 minutes, spray with red drawing ink. Wait about 10 minutes and then lightly press a sheet of waste paper or paper toweling onto the surface of the rubber cement. Lift it up, removing some of the cement. Repeat this several times until almost all the rubber cement is removed. Rub off excess with the fingers.

F. (Drip, Dribble, Drop.) Dip a strip of cloth into a can of black lacquer and dribble it over the surface of the panel. Repeat the process, using medium blue lacquer.

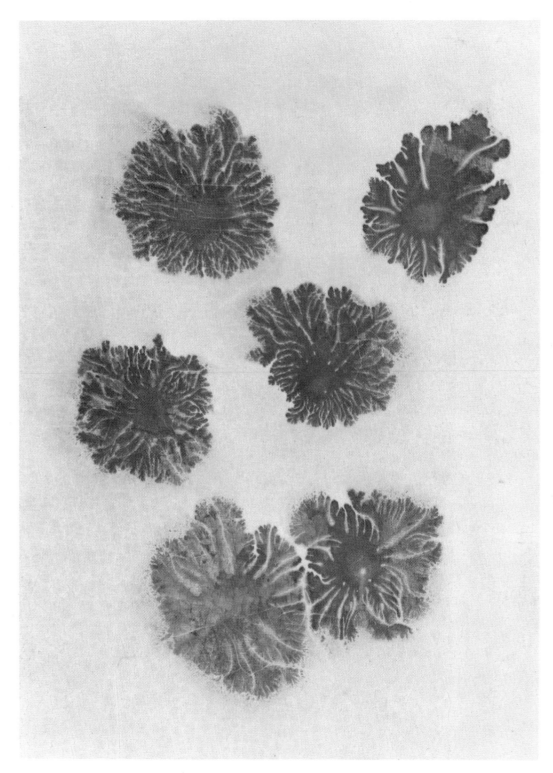

G. (Flowers.) Coat the surface of a panel with sodium silicate, working rapidly because the material dries quickly. Keeping the panel lying flat on a table, place a few drops of vermilion drawing ink (Pelikan) on the surface, using the dropper that comes in the bottle cap. Do not move the panel for a couple of hours; it will then be completely dry.

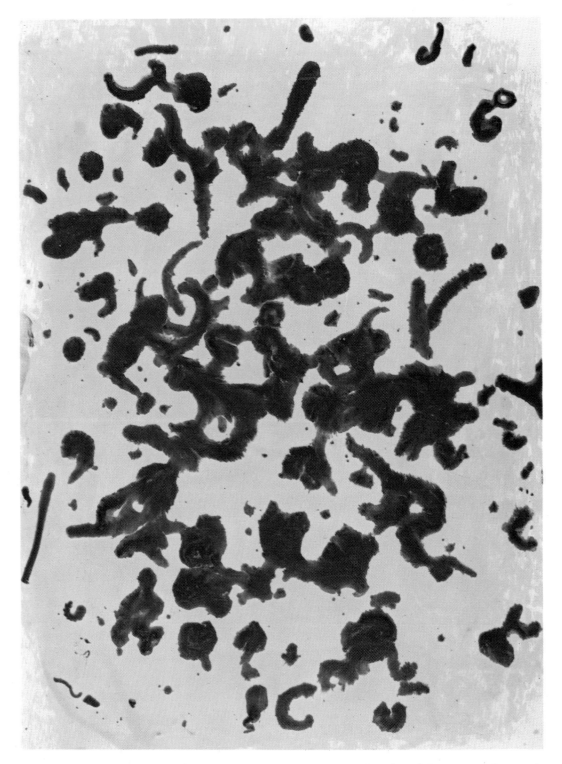

H. (Miscellany.) A variation of Design 170, page 193, with the surface first being rubbed until covered with a yellow crayon, after which dark green crayon shavings are allowed to fall on the surface, and then heated.

76. Cut out a cardboard rectangle 1 ¼″ × 2 ½″. Drop it onto a piece of heavy white drawing paper from a height of 2 feet. With a pencil, outline the rectangle on the drawing paper, wherever it falls. Repeat 26 times. Carefully cut out the shapes formed by the random dropping of the piece of cardboard. Mount the pieces of black paper on a piece of white paper.

Fig. 33.

Fig. 34.

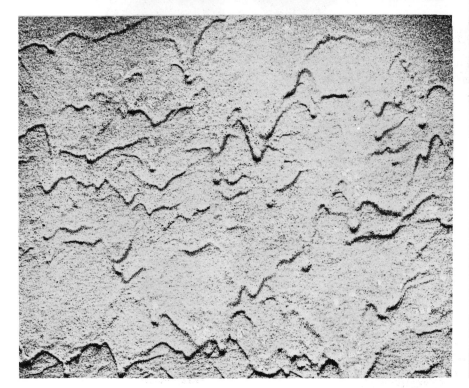

Fig. 35.

Fig. 37.

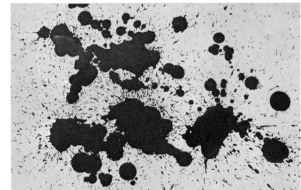

Fig. 36.

splash
and run Designs Formed by

Vigorous Impact and Gravity

Paint has been flicked from a loaded brush, tossed from a bowl, squirted from a squeeze-bottle, heaved in globs, sprayed, or actually shot at a panel by artists in search of new methods of self-expression in painting and the graphic arts. The resulting designs appear aggressive and startling. At a building construction site in any city, many examples of impact-formed designs may be seen in spilled plaster, cement, paint, or asphalt. ■ The designs in this chapter are the result of applying pigments with sufficient force to result in a splash, or the result of gravity pulling pigments downward across a surface.

Fig. 33: Paint can drips. □ **Fig. 34:** Dirty water runs on glass. □ **Fig. 35:** Sagging paint on wall. □ **Fig. 36:** Spilled paint. □ **Fig. 37:** Painting accident on wall. Photos by author.

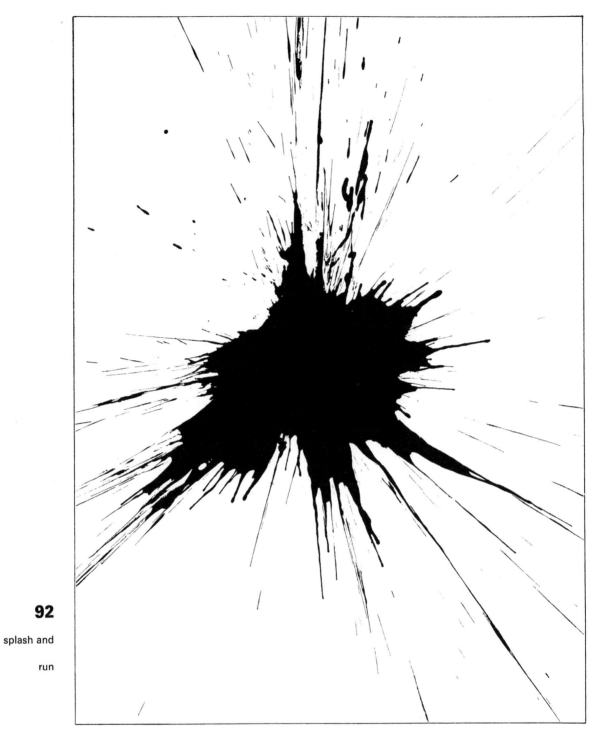

77. A piece of thin, absorbent tissue paper is dipped into India ink and formed into a loose blob of paper and ink, then dropped from a height of 7' onto a white panel laid flat on the floor.

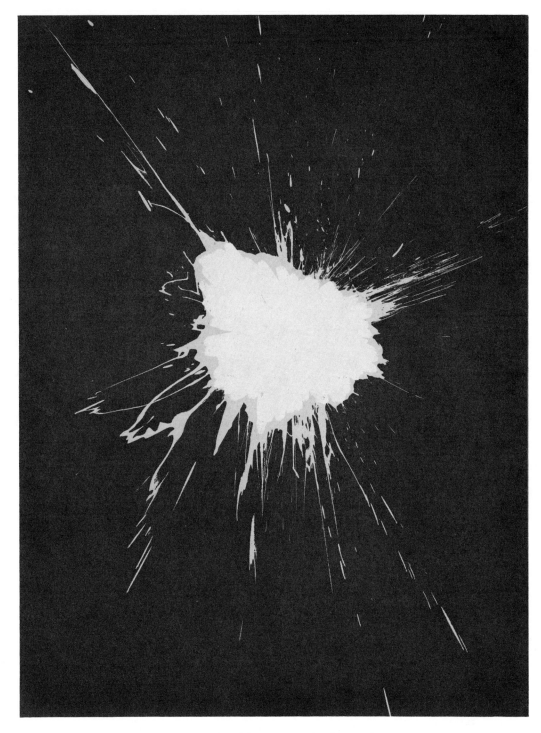

78. Follow the same procedure as for Design 77, but use white showcard color and a black panel.

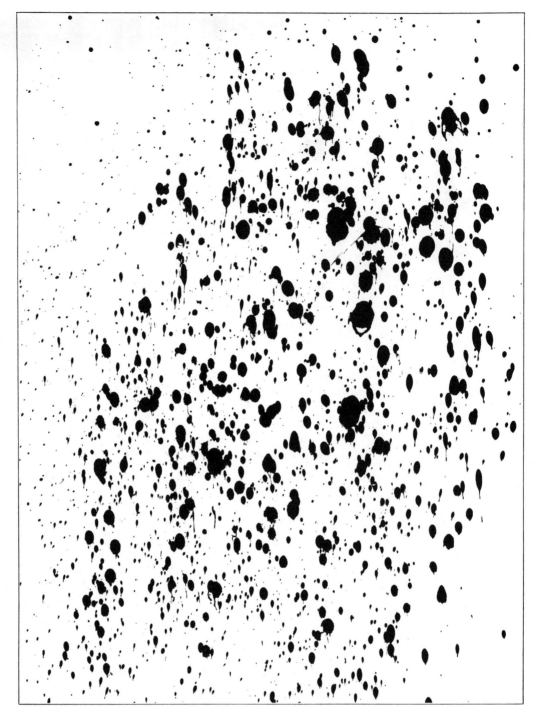

79. A ½" flat brush is dipped into black showcard color. Hold the brush handle by the tip and strike it against a heavy wooden stick held a few inches above a white panel.

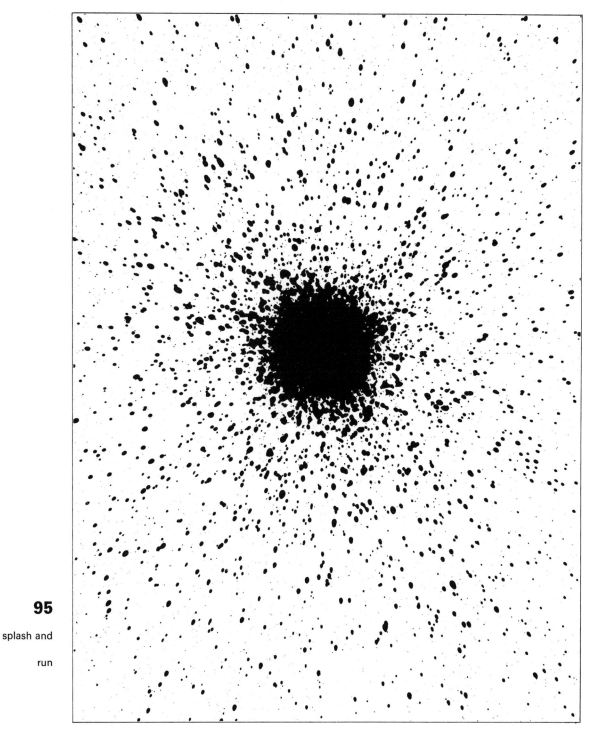

80. This design is simply India ink dropped from the bottle-top dropper on precisely the same spot. The dropper is held against the edge of a table to steady the hand, and the ink is dropped onto a panel laid on the floor below (75 drops).

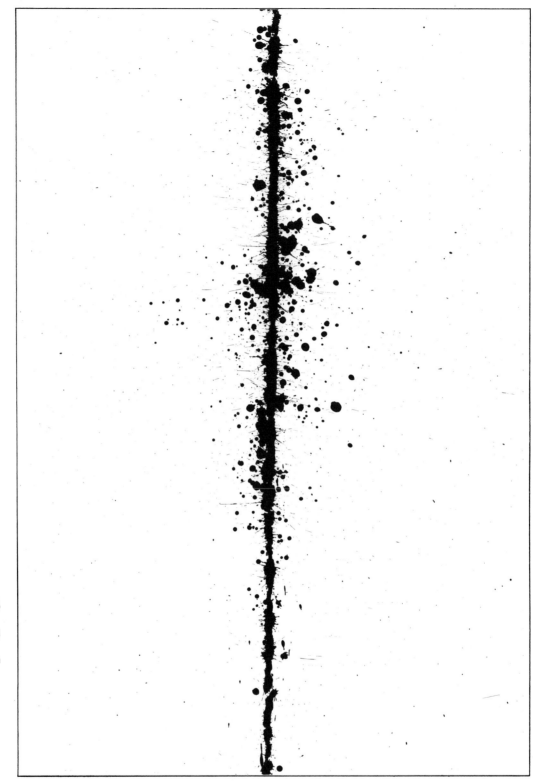

81. A piece of ordinary household string is dipped into India ink. One end of the string is fastened to a thumbtack near the edge of a drawing board and the other end is held firmly just above the surface of the board. A piece of paper is slipped under the string, then the center of the string is pulled slightly upward, in the manner of a taut bowstring, and snapped against the paper.

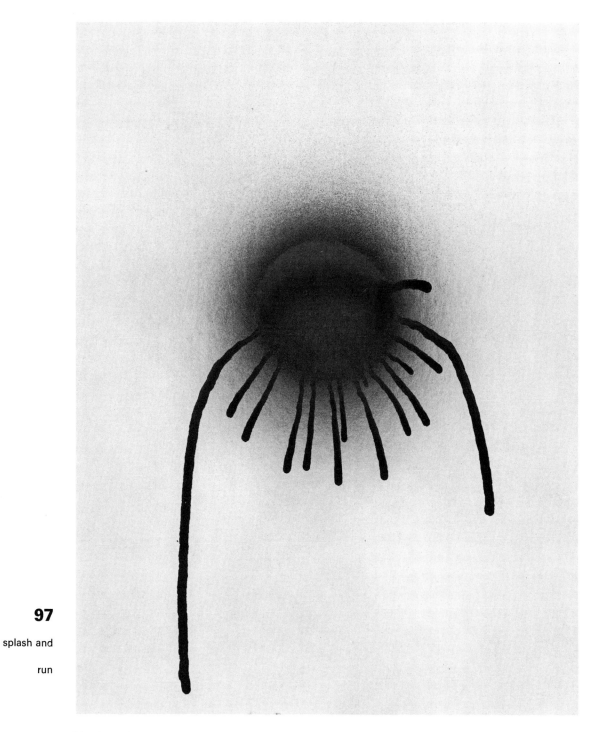

82. Air brush octopus. The panel is held vertically, with the air brush nozzle a few inches from it. Apply the paint until it begins to run.

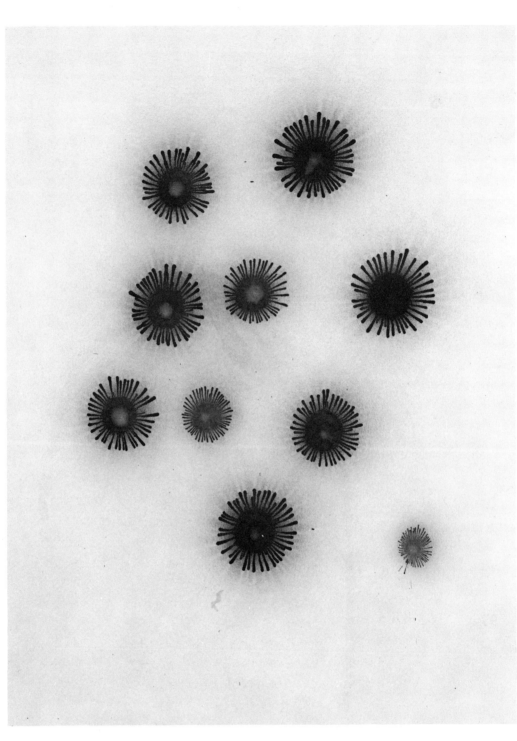

83. Use 25 lbs. air pressure and fill the air brush cup with India ink. Hold the nozzle very close to the panel surface and vertical to it. Make a series of squirts.

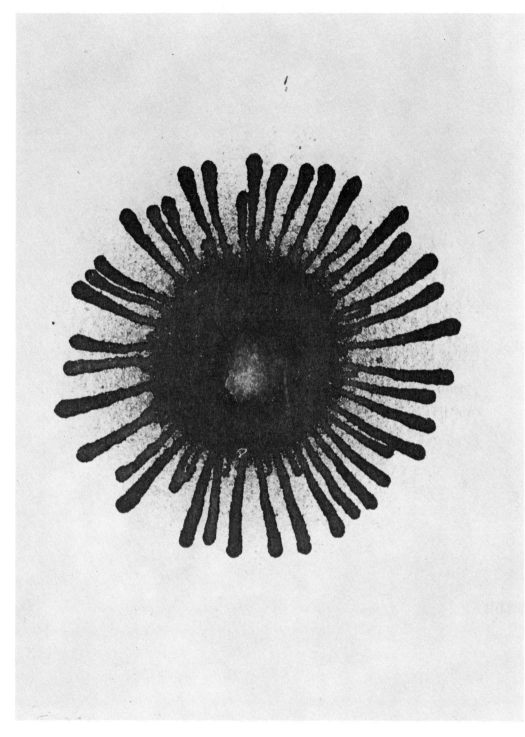

99

splash and

run

84. Enlargement of part of Design 83.

85. Proceed as for Design 83, but hold the air brush at an angle of about 45° with the surface.

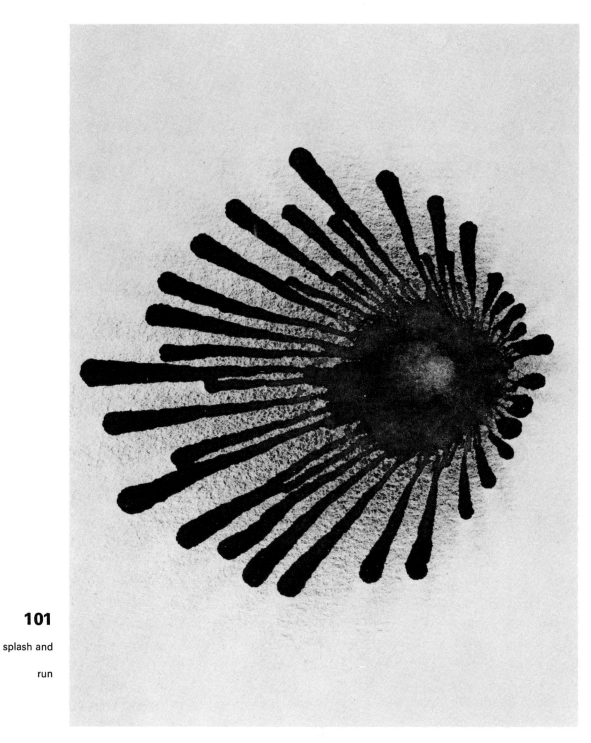

101

splash and

run

86. Enlargement of part of Design 85.

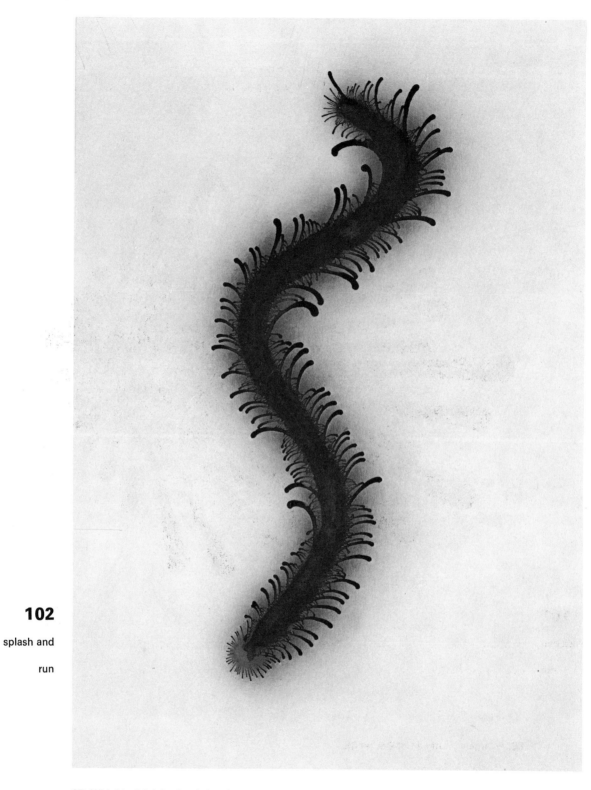

87. With black ink in the air brush cup, and the nozzle held very close to the surface of the paper, a wiggly curve is made, and a centipede is born.

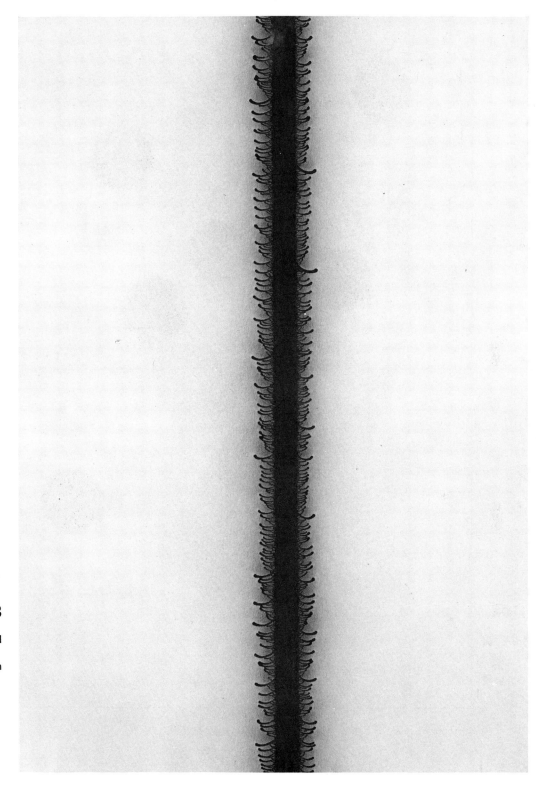

88. A panel is laid flat on a table, and a book is placed at each end, with a ruler resting on the books over the panel, in the manner of a bridge. The bridge is held firmly in place with the left hand and is used to steady the right hand (which holds the air brush, loaded with black ink) as it slides along the ruler, making the design on the panel.

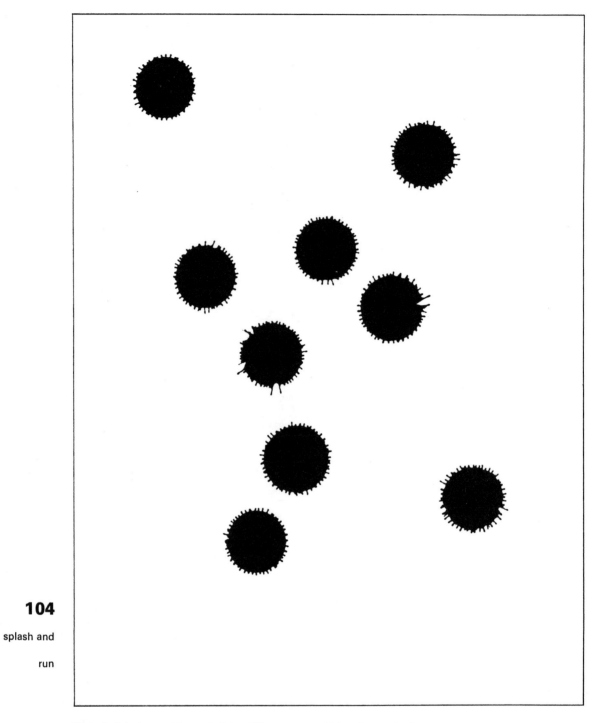

104

splash and

run

89. India ink dropped from a height of 7′ onto a panel lying flat on the floor.

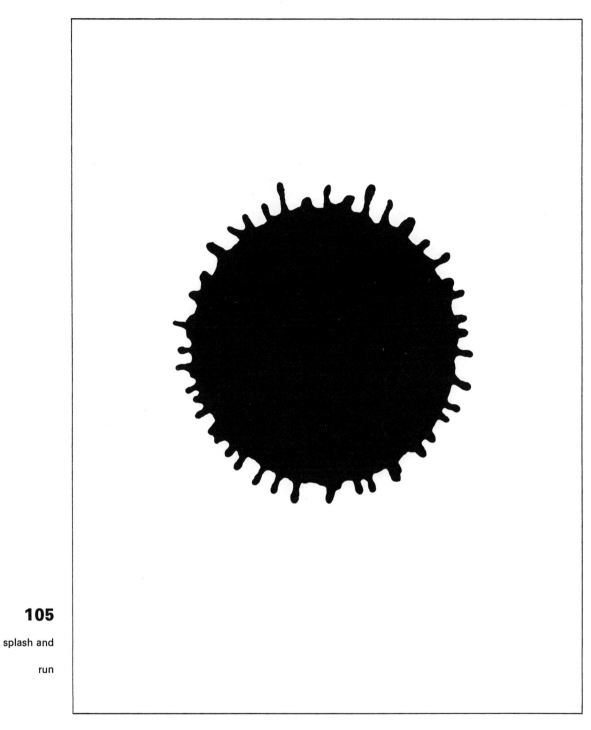

90. Enlargement of part of Design 89.

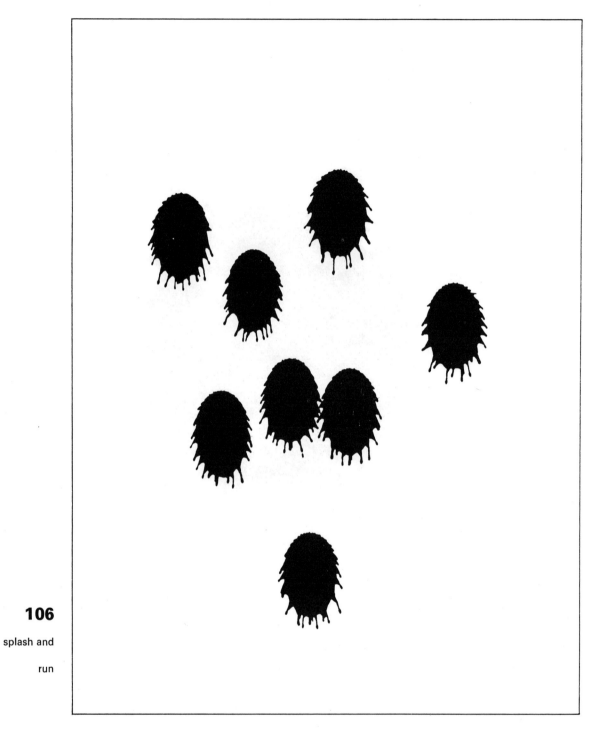

91. The panel is held at a 45° angle, the India ink is dropped from a height of about 4½'—and a group of small and very dirty microbes is born.

92. Enlargement of part of Design 91.

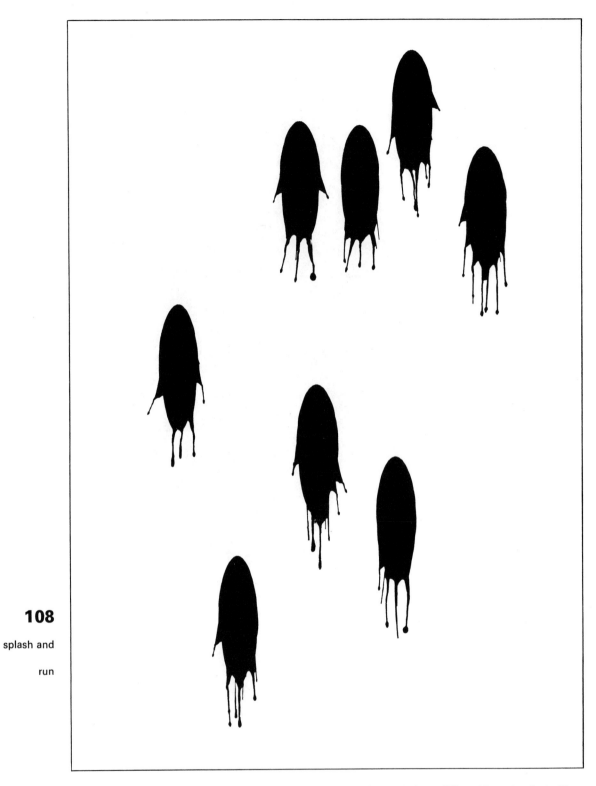

93. The panel is at a steep angle, 60°, and the ink is dropped from a height of 7', making what looks like a family of Martians out for a stroll.

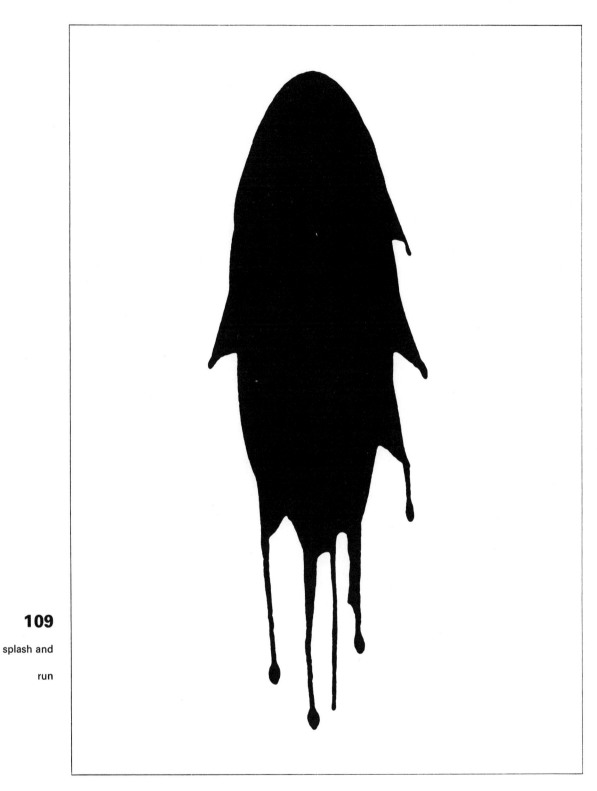

109

splash and

run

94. Enlargement of part of Design 93.

95. The panel is resting at a steep angle, about 60°, and the India ink is dropped from a height of about 3', making a shape that looks like a strangely elongated spoon or a paddle.

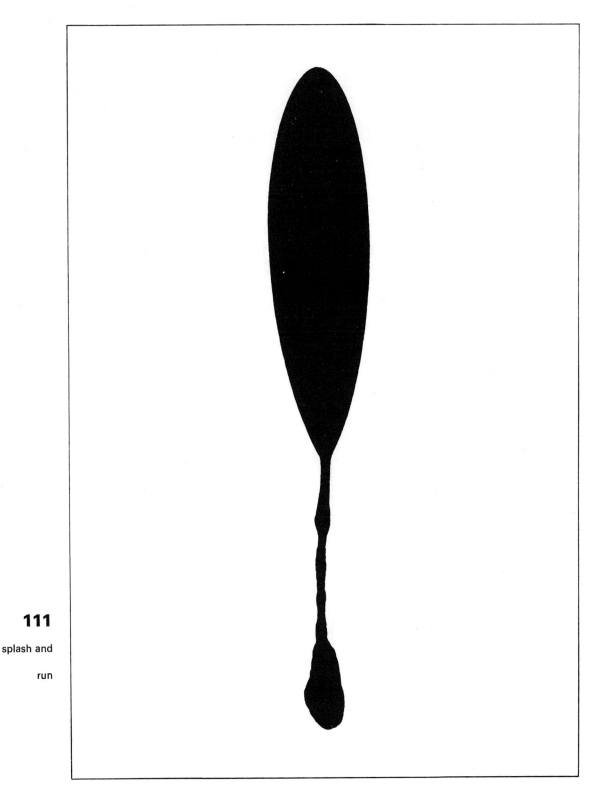

96. Enlargement of part of Design 95.

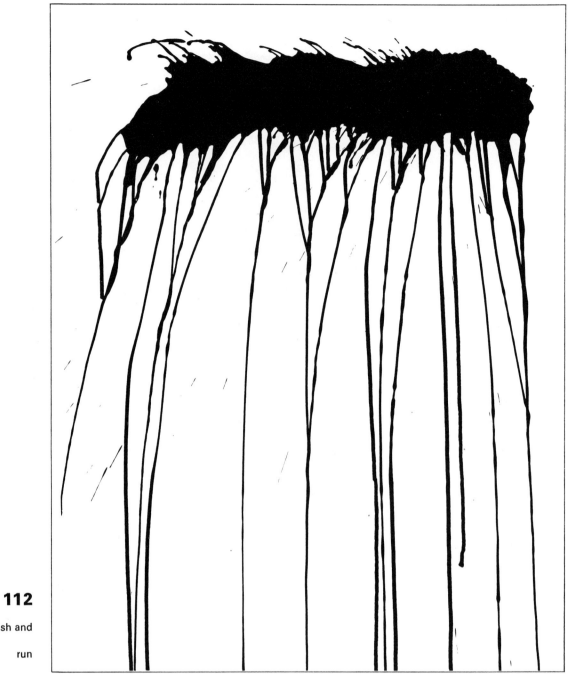

97. A plastic squeeze-bottle with a pointed cap that has a small opening is used to apply the India ink. The method is obvious: the sheet of paper is taped at the corners to a piece of stiff cardboard, and the ink is squirted across the top edge in one quick stroke. The paper is placed against a support at a 45° angle.

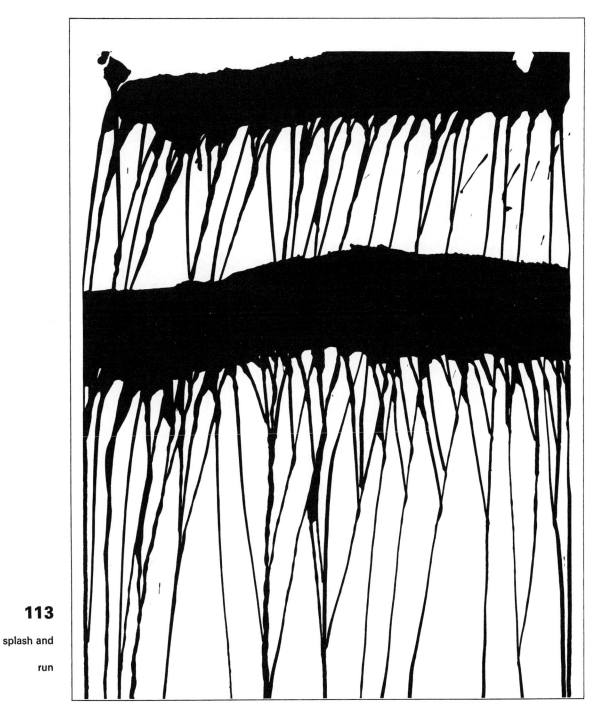

98. Two rows of squirts.

99. Random application of India ink squirts.

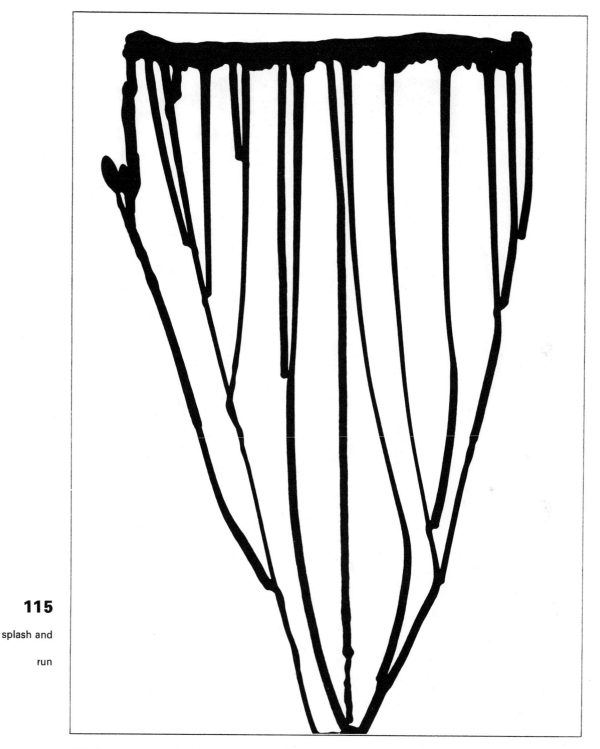

100. A piece of two-ply Bristol paper is taped along the upper edge to a piece of stiff cardboard. The two lower corners are bent forward and toward each other until they touch, and are then taped together, thus forming a sort of half-funnel. India ink is squirted along the top edge in one quick stroke, and it runs together near the bottom of the half-funnel.

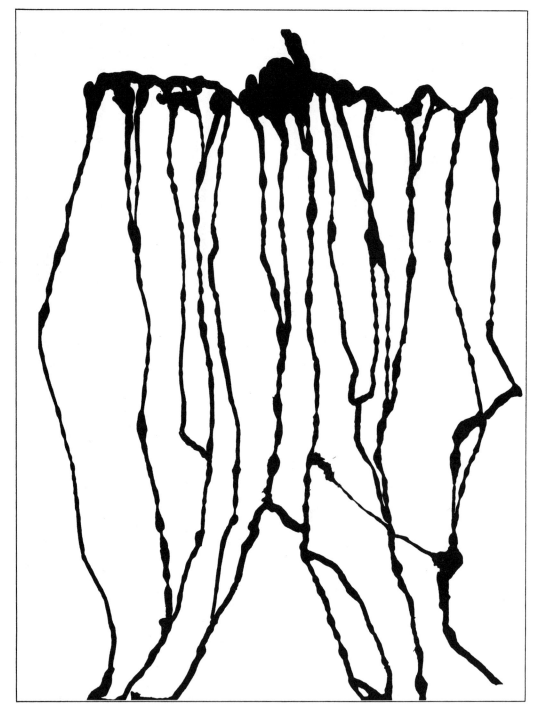

101. A piece of two-ply Bristol paper is crumpled into a small ball, then unfolded and taped down to a piece of cardboard. When the ink is squirted across the top edge, the folds and wrinkles in the paper cause an irregular and hesitant flow of ink.

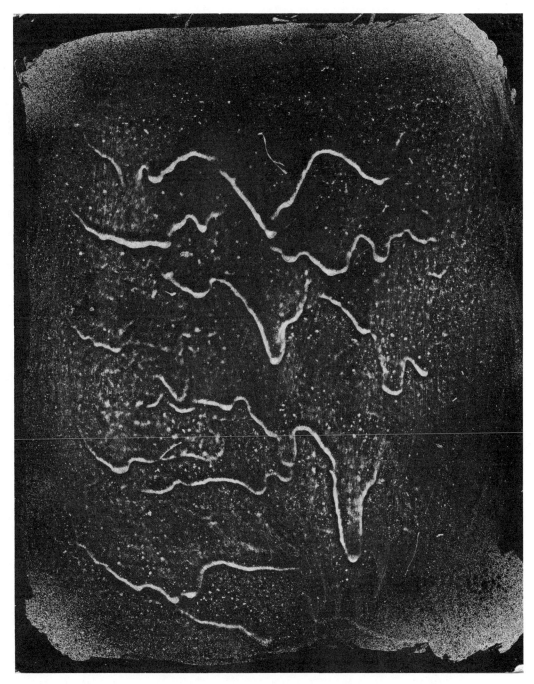

102. Hold a panel almost vertically. Starting at the bottom and using a loaded brush, apply white lacquer in bands across the surface, allowing the lacquer to flow downward. Tilt the panel as necessary to have some control over the flow. Lay panel flat and allow to dry. Spray with black enamel or lacquer. When dry, sand lightly with very fine sandpaper.

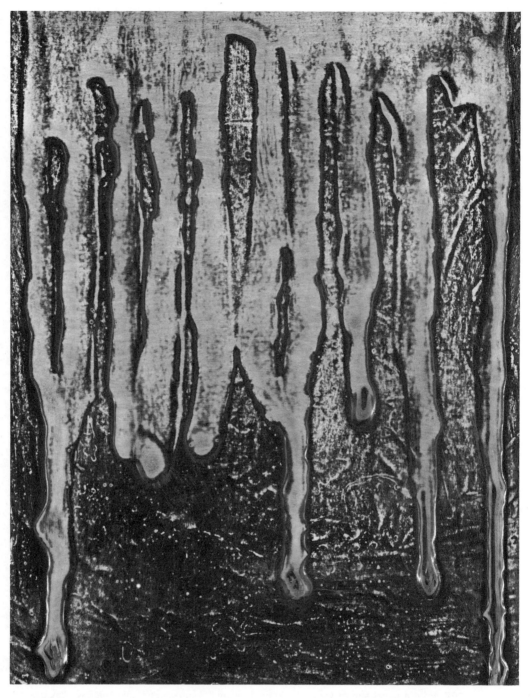

103. A panel is given a thin coat of Elmer's Glue-All, and is then placed against a support almost vertically. More glue is dribbled along the top edge until it runs down the face of the panel, which is then allowed to dry. India ink is brushed over the surface and again allowed to dry. The surface is then rubbed with fine sandpaper to reveal the design.

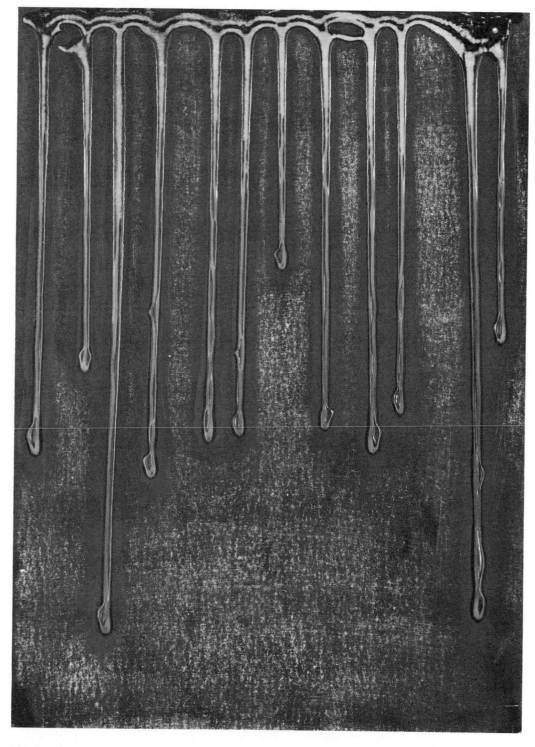

104. The same procedure is used as for Design 103, except that the glue is dribbled directly onto the bare panel, without the preliminary coat of glue.

Fig. 38.

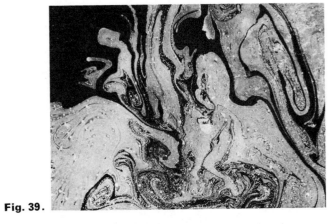

Fig. 39.

Fig. 40.

Fig. 41.

flow
and swirl

"Marble Effect"

A body of water is seldom completely at rest; various currents are continually rolling and turning. In clear water the movement is often invisible, but if the surface is covered with dust, algae, small sticks, or pollen, the curling eddies become clearly evident. The pattern formed on the surface of liquids is remarkably like that on the surface of certain types of polished marble slabs. ■ Manufacturers use this phenomenon to produce marble designs on wooden panels or other display objects. They simply float a small amount of paint on the surface of a large pan of water, agitate it slightly, dip the object to be marbleized into the water, then deftly remove it, with the marble design permanently attached to the surface. This technique is also used to make designs on fabrics, end-papers of expensive books, and imitation marble slabs.

Fig. 38: Eddies in dirty water. □ **Fig. 39:** Imitation marble panel. □ **Fig. 40:** Flowing lava during an eruption of Mauna Loa in Hawaii. U.S. Navy photo. □ **Fig. 41:** Marble panel on building front. Photos for Figs. 38, 39 and 41 by author.

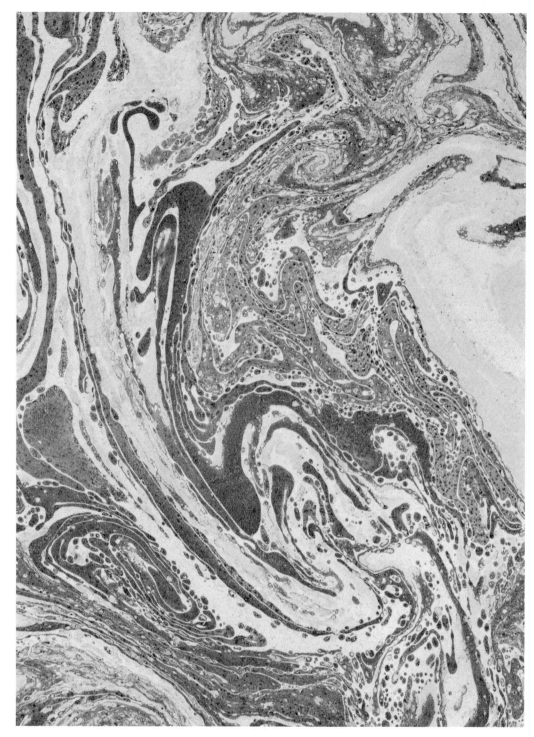

105. The method used in preparing this design was also used for all the others in this chapter: A small amount of pigment in an oily medium is floated on the surface of a pan of water. If the water is stirred or slightly disturbed with a spoon or paddle, the pigments will form a marble-like design, its complexity being determined by how much the water is moved and what types of pigment and medium are used. The surface of the water is watched until a particularly desirable design appears, then an illustration board panel is quickly lowered into the water, white side down. The panel is tilted slightly while being lowered in order to prevent bubbles from forming. When the panel is completely submerged, it is tilted and slipped out of the water; the design adheres to the surface. Place the panel on newspapers to dry overnight. The pan used for all the designs in this chapter was 12" × 16" × 6" deep. [continued]

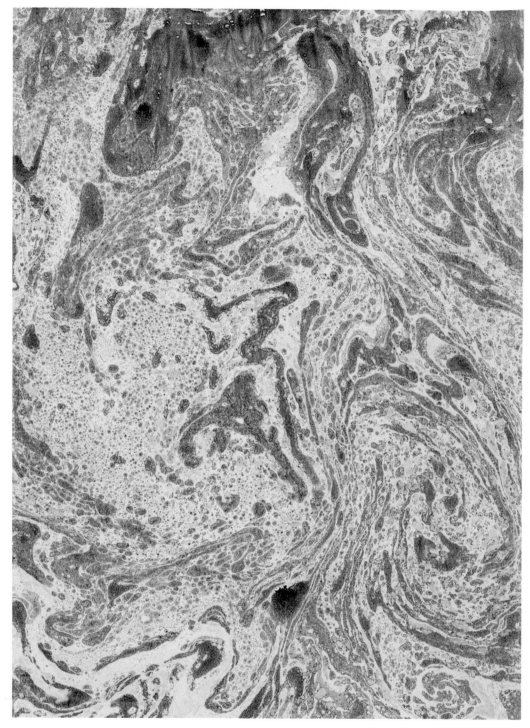

123

flow and swirl

106. Variation of Design 105.

[Plate 105, continued] The water was about 4″ deep, and the panels measured 7½″ × 10″. The pigment used in this first illustration was Grumbacher's Ivory Black Oil Color, thoroughly mixed with enough kerosene to make it flow freely. A separate container of Titanium White was also mixed with kerosene. Small quantities of each of these pigments were poured onto the surface of the water and slightly agitated.

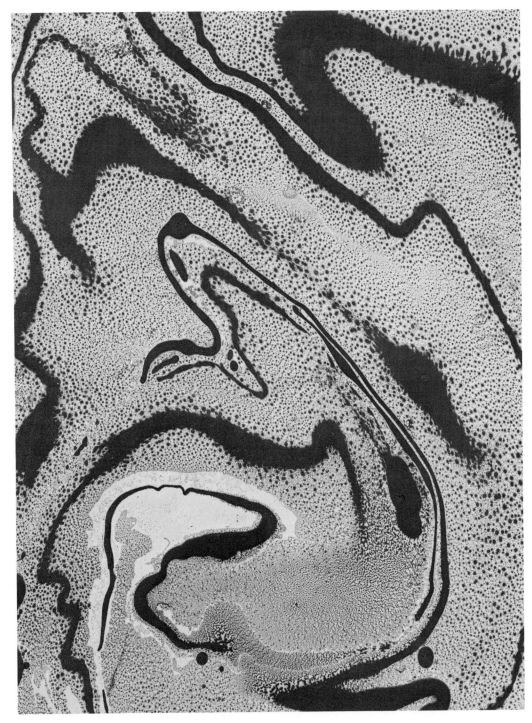

107. For this design black Japan color was used on a white panel (Skoler Display Art Flat Poster Color).

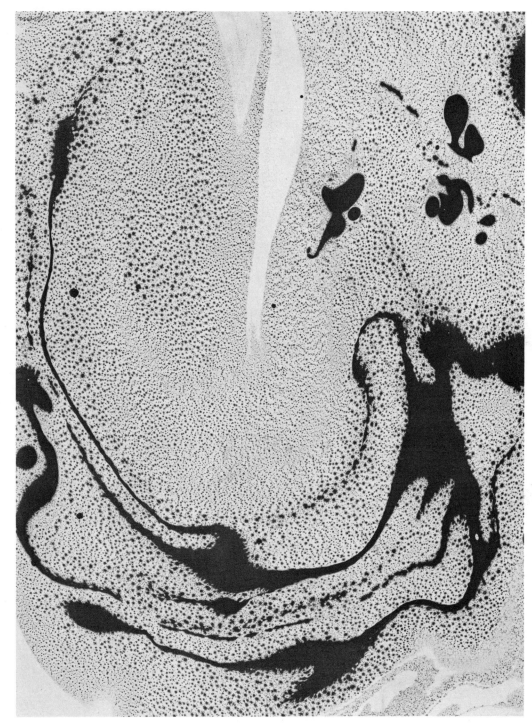

108. Variation of Design 107.

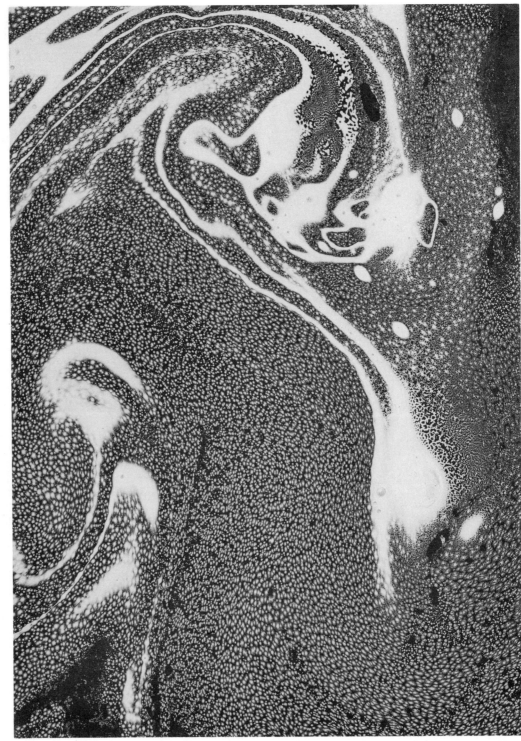

109. White Japan color on a panel that has been sprayed with black enamel (Skoler Display Art Flat Poster Color).

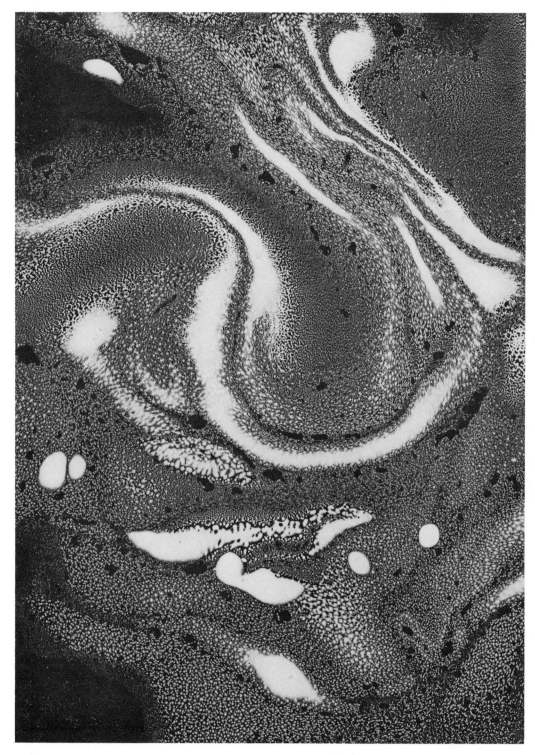

110. Variation of Design 109.

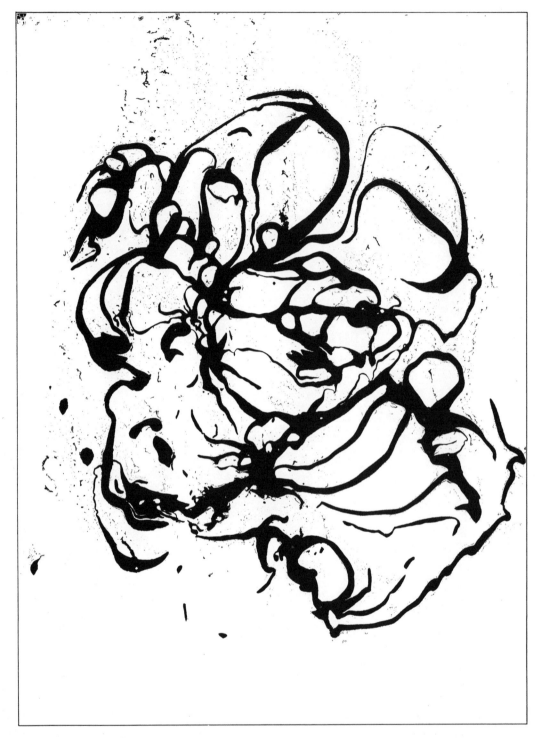

111. Variation of Design 107. Use Japan color. Add one teaspoon of liquid detergent (Vel) to the water and stir well before dribbling the paint onto the surface of the water. Let the paint dribble in a random Pollock-type pattern, and it will form characteristic shapes quite different from those obtained when no detergent is used.

129

flow and swirl

112. Variation of Design 111.

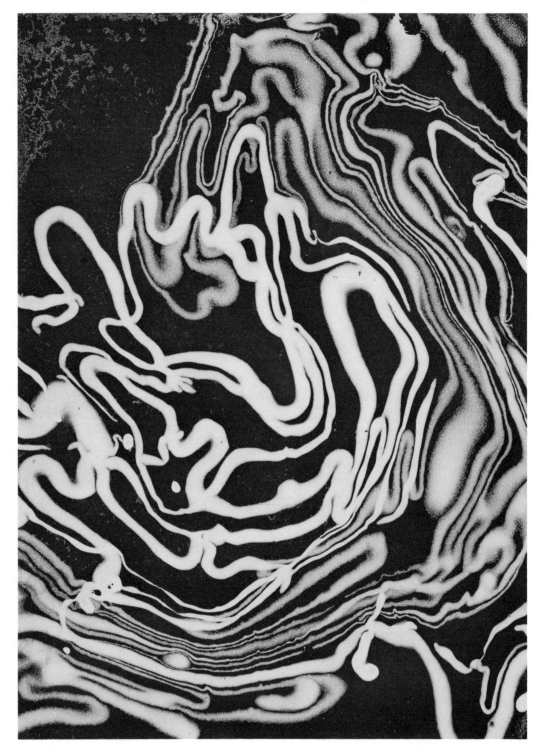

130

flow and swirl

113. Use the same procedure as for Design 111, with detergent in the water, but use a black panel with white Japan color.

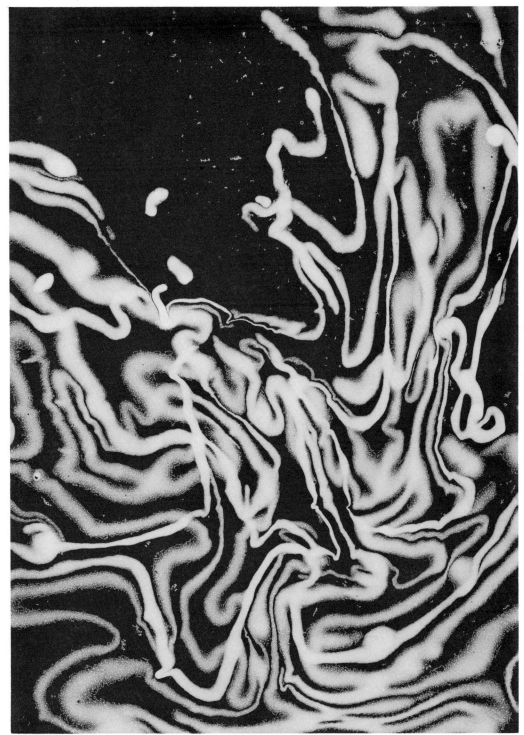

131

flow and swirl

114. Variation of Design 113.

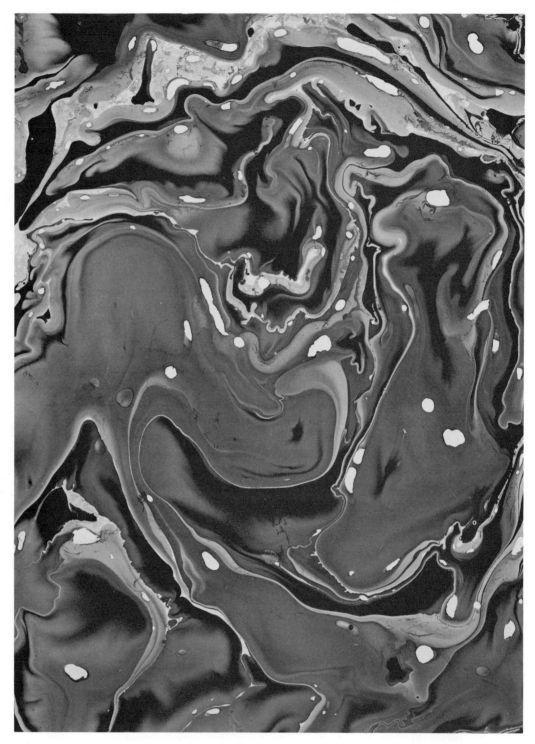

115. Black enamel on white panel (Super-Tex Odorless Enamel).

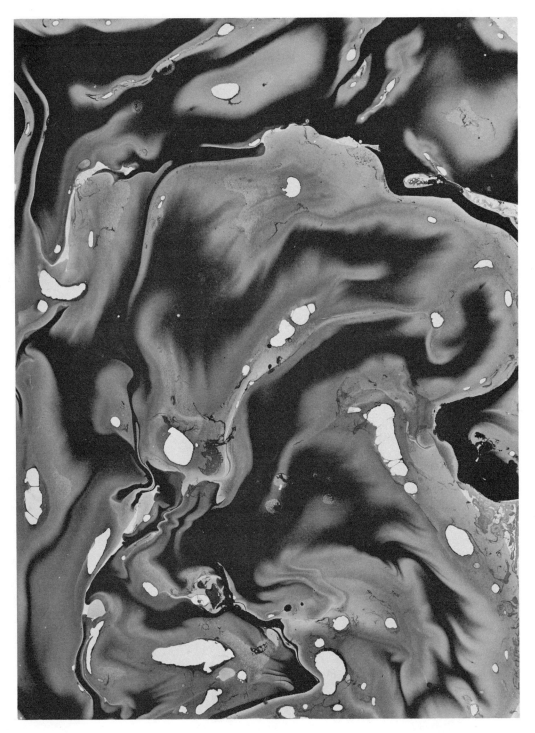

133

flow and swirl

116. Variation of Design 115.

117. White enamel on black panel (Super-Tex Odorless Enamel).

118. Felt pen ink on white panel (Marsh T-Grade Black for felt-point pens).

Fig. 42.

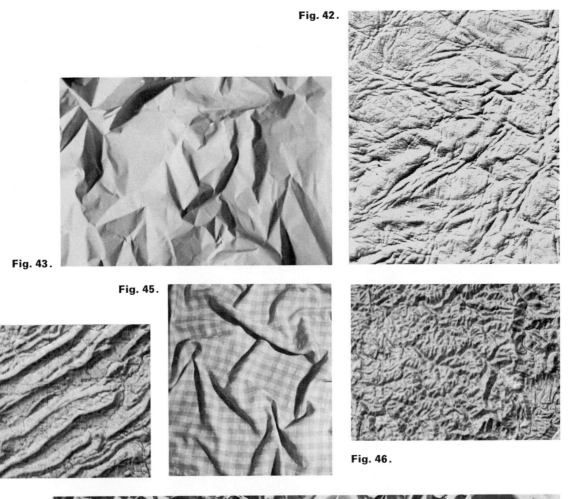

Fig. 43.

Fig. 45.

Fig. 44.

Fig. 46.

Fig. 47.

wrinkles
and folds Folding
and Bending of Surfaces

Innumerable portraits by artists of the traditional-realist schools of painting reveal the eye-appeal of folds and wrinkles. Our eyes seem to delight in following the graceful curves of folds in soft materials, the swift lines and angles in stiffer fabrics, and the highlights, shadows, and designs made by both wrinkles and folds. ■ Painters like Velásquez or Titian often gave much attention to depicting the folds of satins, silks, and velvets. Of course, the person being painted was the real subject matter, but the artist was keenly aware of the visual interest of folds and wrinkles as objects of beauty in their own right. Nowadays, thin films of plastic and metal foils make wrinkles and folds with highlights that would astonish artists of earlier times. Aerial photographs reveal wrinkles in the earth's skin not much different in appearance from wrinkles that can be made on paper.

Fig. 42: Leather surface. □ **Fig. 43:** Crumpled paper. □ **Fig. 44:** Mountains on relief map. **Fig. 45:** Cloth folds. □ **Fig. 46:** Mountains on relief map. □ **Fig. 47:** Crinkled aluminum foil. Photos by author.

119. A piece of tracing paper, 9" × 12", is crumpled into a ball. It is then unfolded and taped at the corners onto a table. Black ink is airbrushed horizontally across the surface.

120. Same procedure as for Design 119, but use bond paper instead.

121. Same procedure as for Design 119, but use bond paper crushed lengthwise.

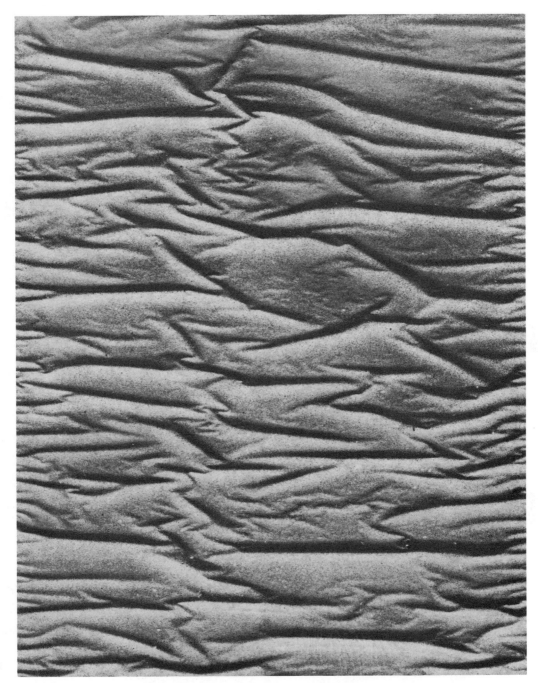

141

wrinkles and

folds

122. A piece of tracing paper ("The Parchment" brand), 8½" × 11", is taped firmly around the edges to a piece of stiff cardboard. The tracing paper is then soaked with water; this causes the paper to wrinkle. Immediately, while the paper is still quite wet, airbrush black ink horizontally across the surface. When the paper has dried, cut apart from tape and mount on stiff material.

123. Follow the same procedure as for Design 122, but use a heavier tracing paper (Albanene).

143

wrinkles and

folds

124. A piece of thin tracing paper is soaked in water and then pinned onto a line to dry. After it is com- pletely dry, spray black across the surface with air brush. Mount on stiff material.

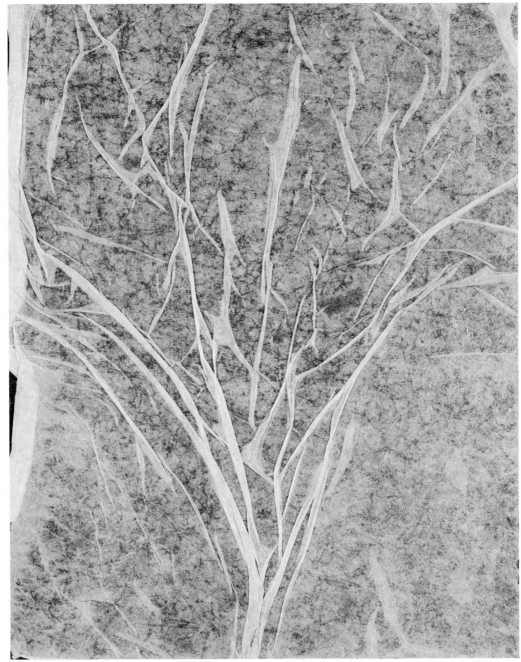

144

wrinkles and

folds

125. With Elmer's Glue-All, thin wet rice paper is glued onto a black panel.

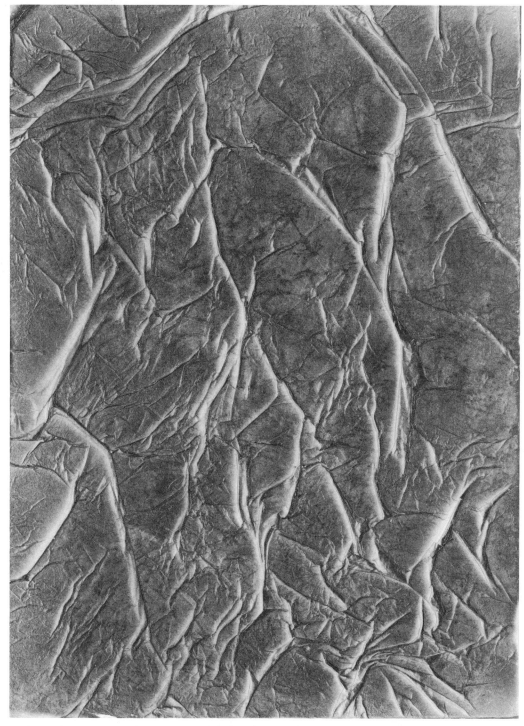

145

wrinkles and

folds

126. Wet rice paper glued onto a white panel. When this is dry, black ink is airbrushed across the surface.

127. A piece of newsprint, 18" × 24", is crumpled into a ball and pressed against a piece of cardboard that has a thick wet coat of black showcard color on it. The crumpled paper is then pressed against the center of a white panel, transferring the design.

147

wrinkles and

folds

128. Variation of Design 127.

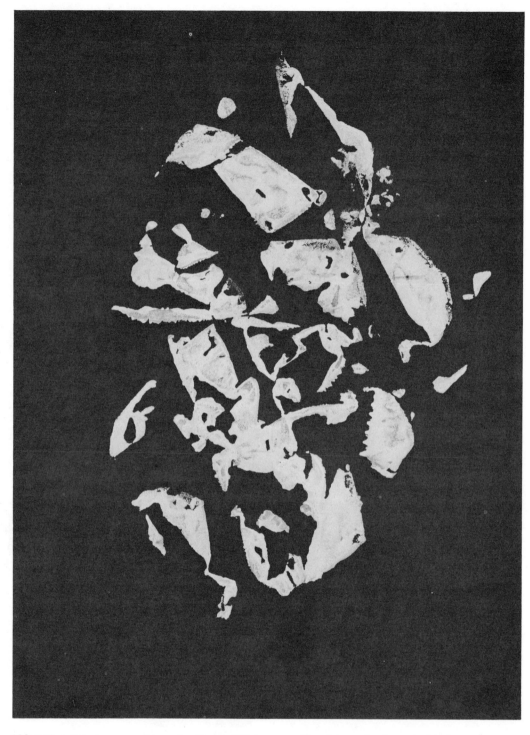

129. Follow the same procedure as for Design 127, but use white showcard color and a black panel.

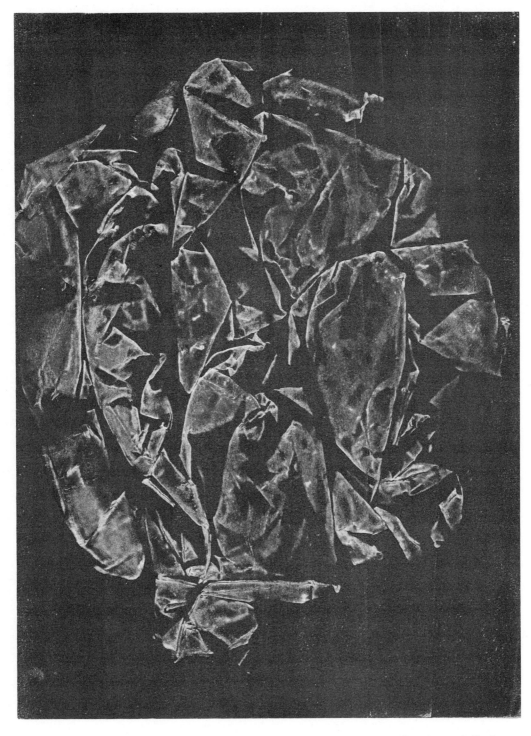

130. Using a rubber brayer (hand-roller), coat the surface of a piece of illustration board with black finger paint. Roll the paint horizontally and vertically across the face of the panel until an even coat is obtained. Quickly take a large piece of newsprint, crumple it into a large ball, and press it firmly onto the still-wet surface. Remove carefully to avoid smearing. A similar effect can be obtained by using black oil paint in place of the finger paint.

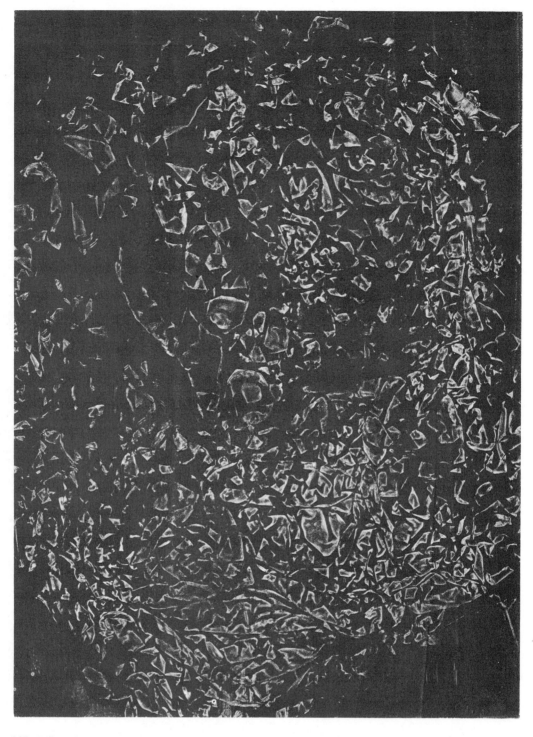

150

wrinkles and

folds

131. Follow the same procedure as for Design 130, but in place of the crumpled newsprint use a crumpled piece of aluminum foil. It is necessary to press very hard to produce an image.

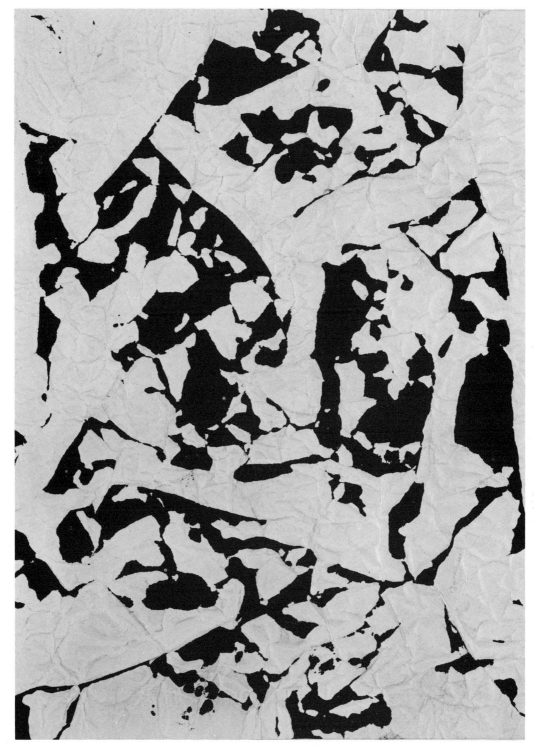

132. A piece of ordinary mimeograph or bond paper is wrinkled into a ball, then partly unfolded and pressed onto a piece of cardboard that is coated with wet showcard color. The paint picked up by the paper is allowed to dry, then the paper is flattened and mounted onto stiff cardboard.

133. Wrinkle black paper into a ball, then unfold it and press it onto a board coated with wet white paint. After drying, mount. Since the black paper is heavier, it forms larger designs of a slightly different character.

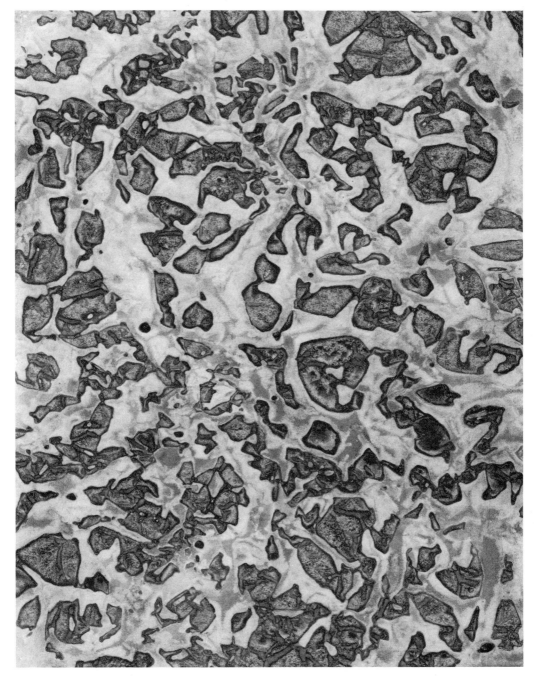

134. A mixture of black showcard color and water is made in the proportion of 20 teaspoons of water to 1 teaspoon of paint. A piece of illustration board is held under a faucet for about 15 seconds, until the surface of the panel is well soaked with water. Lay the panel flat on some newspapers on a table, and give it a coat of the water-paint mixture. Quickly crumple a piece of wax paper into a ball, then unfold it and place it on the wet painted surface, patting it lightly until it lies reasonably flat. Allow to dry for about 2 hours, and then remove wax paper.

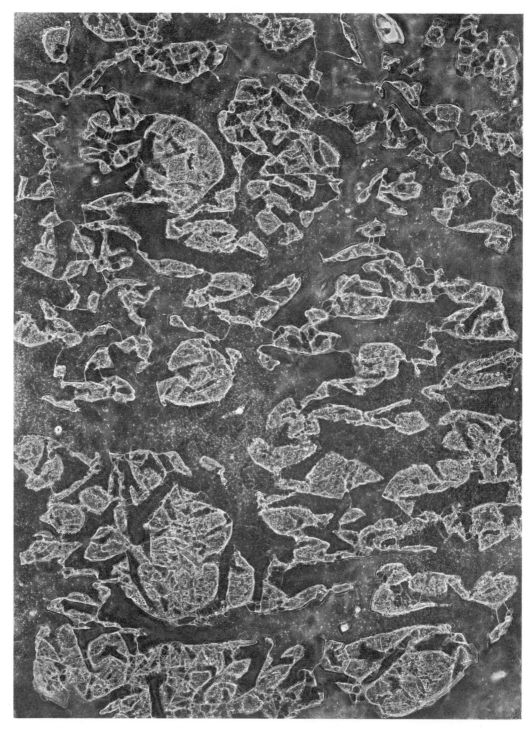

135. Illustration board is sprayed with black enamel. After it is thoroughly dry, follow the same procedure as for Design 134, also using crumpled wax paper and white showcard color.

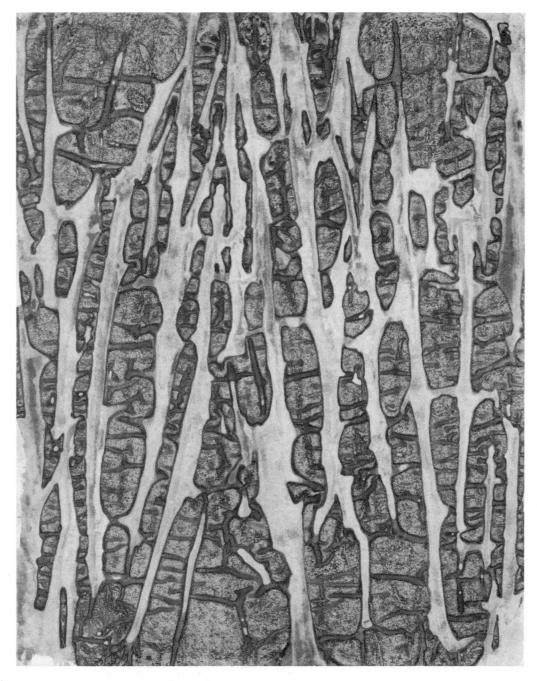

136. Follow same steps as for Design 134, but instead of crumpling the wax paper into a ball, roll it into a tube, and crush the tube in the hands so that the wrinkles run lengthwise along the paper. Unroll the paper and place it on the water-paint surface as before.

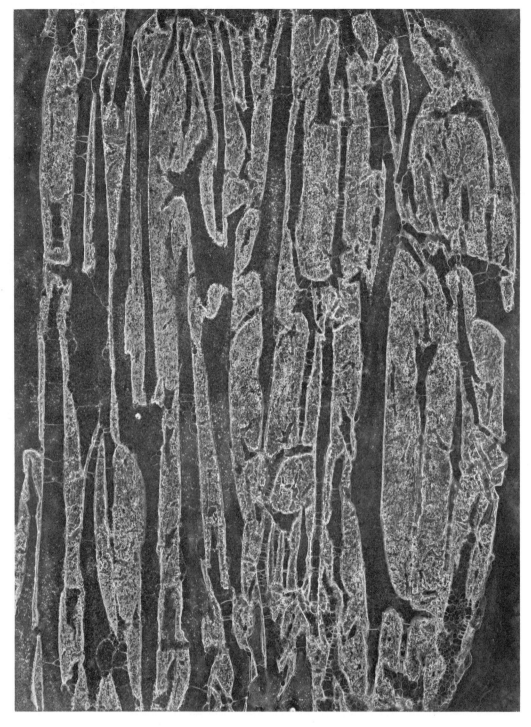

137. Illustration board is sprayed with black enamel. After it is thoroughly dry, follow the same procedure as for Design 136, again using wax paper rolled into a tube, then crumpled lengthwise, and white show-card color.

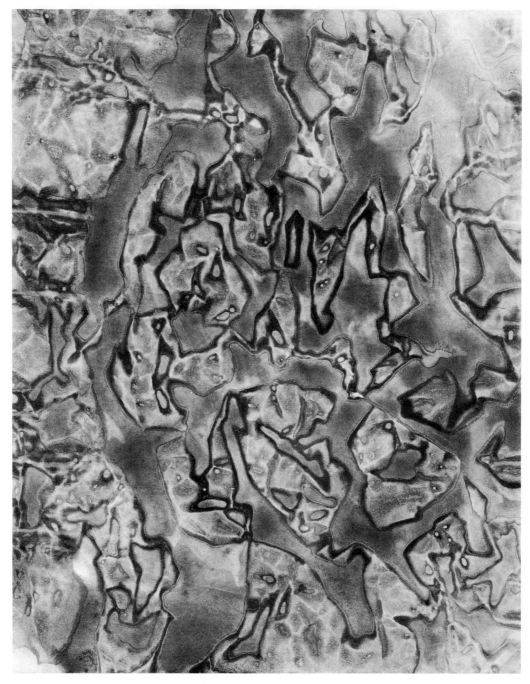

138. Follow the same procedure as for Design 134, but instead of using wax paper, use a crumpled sheet of mimeograph or typing paper.

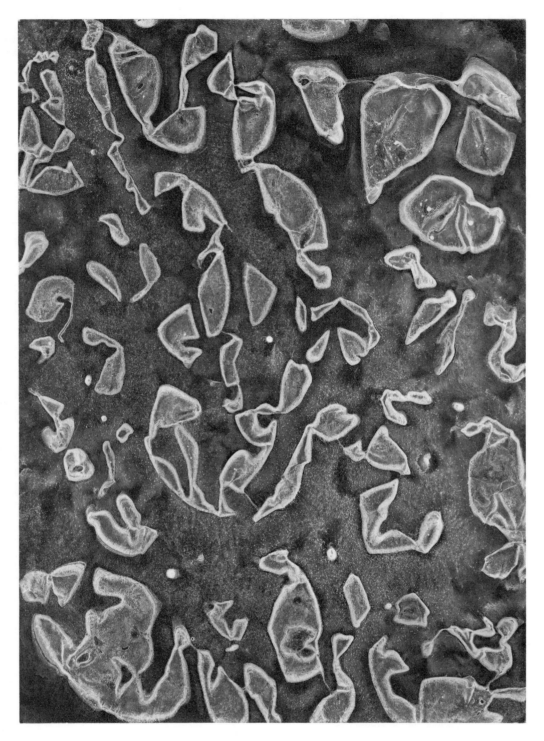

139. Illustration board is sprayed with black enamel. After it is thoroughly dry, the same procedure is followed as for Design 138, except that white show-card color is used in place of black.

140. Mix one tablespoon of showcard color with three parts of water. Take a sheet of Saran Wrap or other thin transparent food wrapping material and apply a few drops of detergent to each side; then apply water to both sides in the kitchen sink. (The detergent will prevent the Saran Wrap from repelling the water.) Place the wrinkled wrapping material on a still-wet illustration board panel which has been coated with the mixture of water and poster color. Lay the panel flat on a table and allow to dry overnight. Carefully remove the wrapping material and spray the dry design with Krylon.

160

wrinkles and

folds

141. Variation of Design 140.

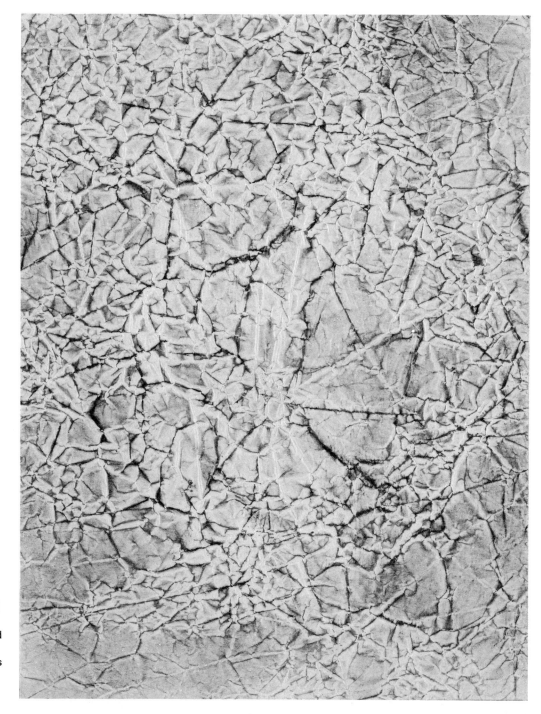

142. Crumple a piece of medium-weight tracing paper into a ball and then unfold carefully to prevent tearing. Lay it on a piece of newspaper and hold it in place while rubbing the wrinkled surface with carbon paper. Mount on white cardboard and spray with fixative.

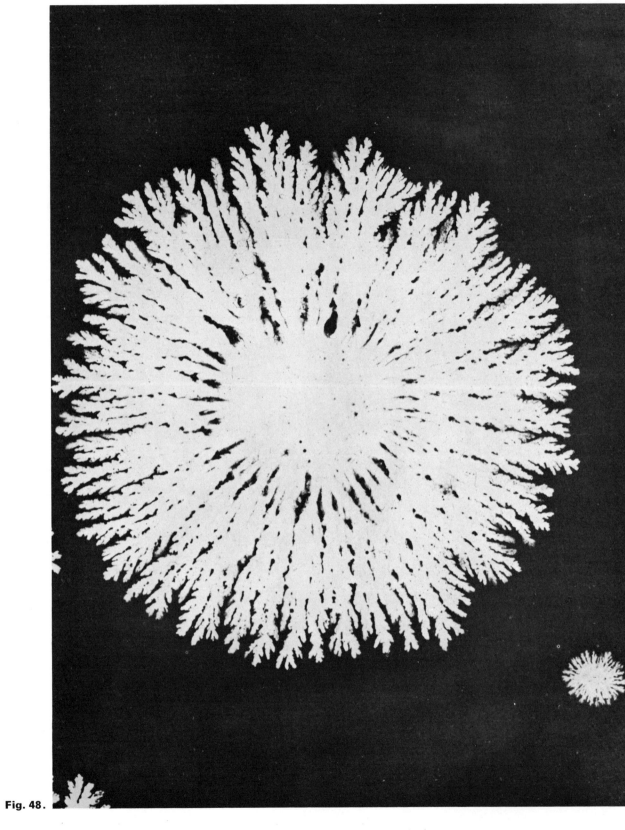

Fig. 48.

flowers Patterns Formed by

Drops of Pigment on a Coated Surface

When a drop of liquid falls onto a flat surface it makes a splash, and that may be the end of it. However, if the liquid happens to be Dr. Ph. Martin's Water Color and the surface a piece of illustration board covered with a thin coat of water-base poster color, the drop of liquid forms an intricate flower-like design that is a thing of real beauty. The following illustrations are the result of various combinations of liquids dropped onto coated surfaces. Some of the more interesting ones are enlarged.

Fig. 48: Another shot of Design 146. All the enlarged photographs in this chapter are by James R. Dunlop, Inc., Washington, D. C.

163

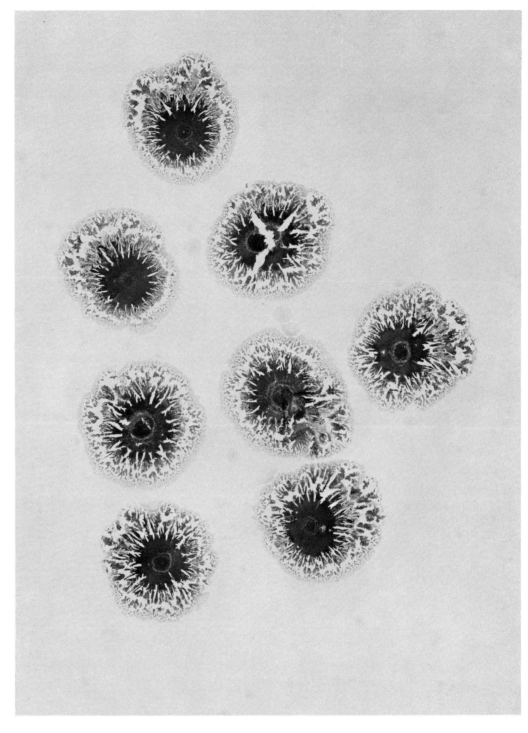

143. A piece of illustration board is given a thin coat of white showcard color. While the paint is still wet, violet Higgins Drawing Ink is carefully dropped onto the surface from a height of about 6″ and left undisturbed until it dries.

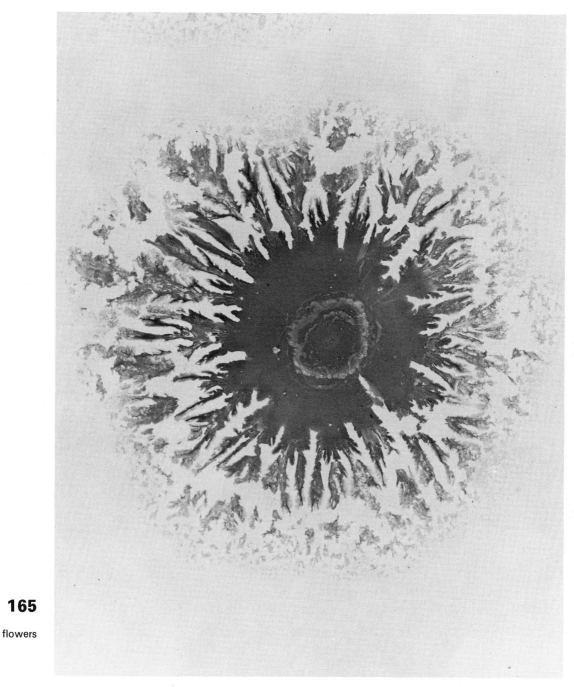

144. Enlargement of part of Design 143.

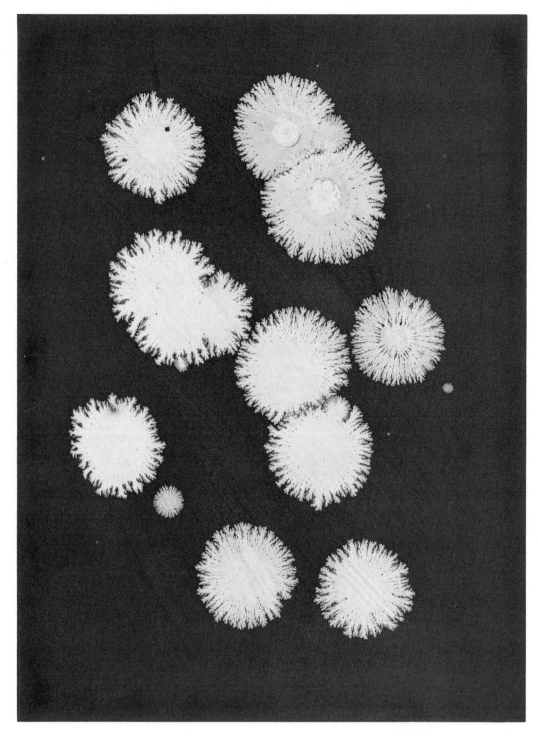

145. A piece of illustration board is painted with a thin coat of black showcard color. A small amount of white showcard color is diluted with an equal amount of water and dropped from a brush or medicine dropper onto the surface of the still-wet black paint. Do not move the board until it is dry.

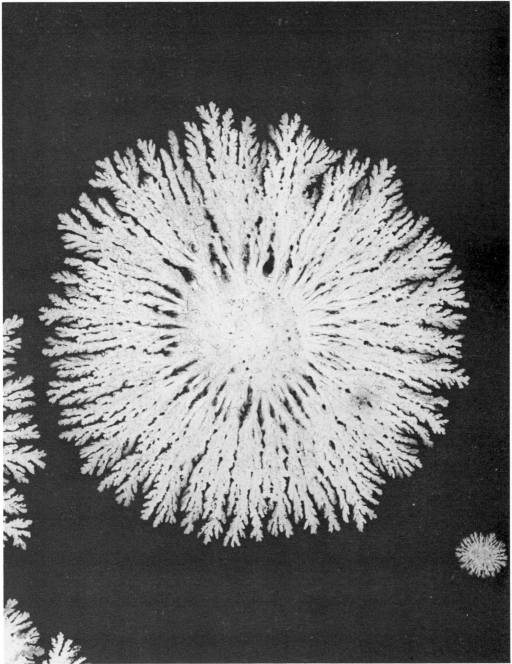

146. Enlargement of part of Design 145.

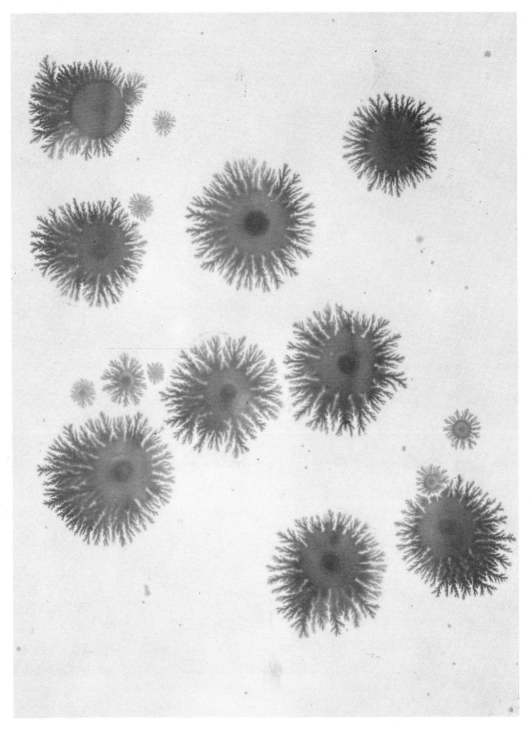

147. Follow the same procedure as for Design 145, using Dr. Ph. Martin's Ultramarine Water Color in place of drawing ink.

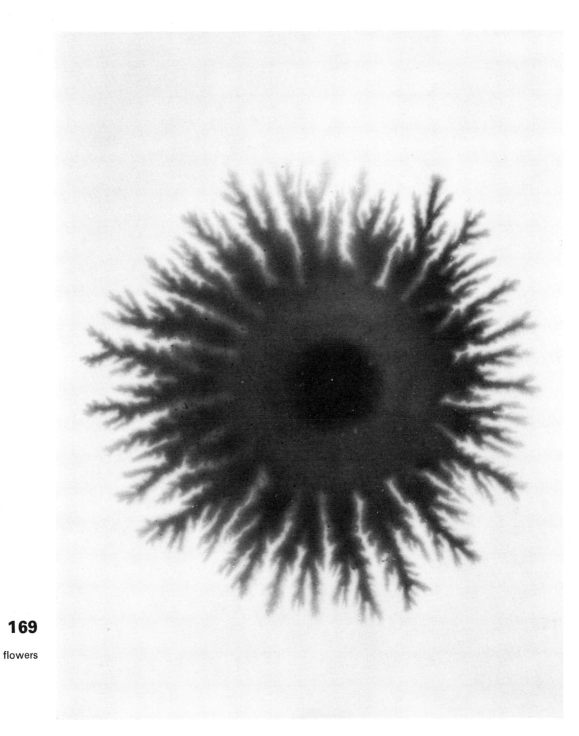

148. Enlargement of part of Design 147.

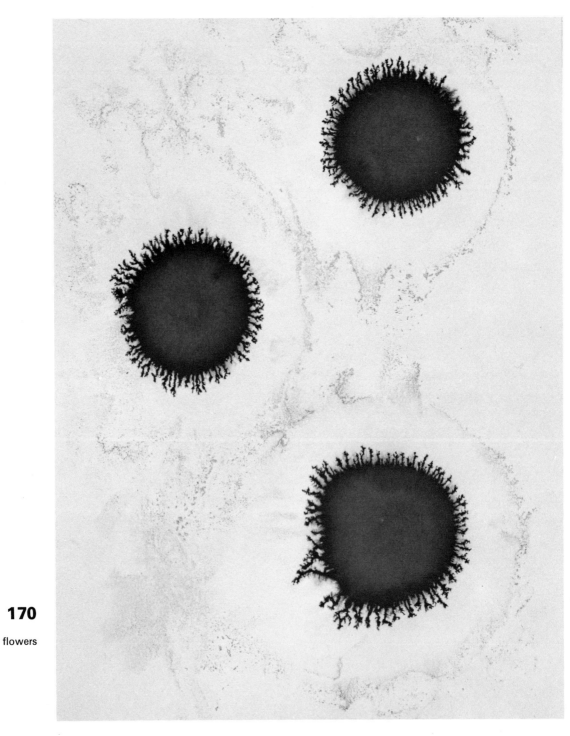

149. Take a piece of two-ply Bristol board and wet both sides thoroughly by holding it under a faucet. Hold by the tip of one corner over the sink to allow some of the water to run off. When the paper is still quite wet and drops are still falling off into the sink, lay it flat on a table or floor, and quickly place a few drops of India ink on the surface, using the dropper on the bottle cap. Allow to dry.

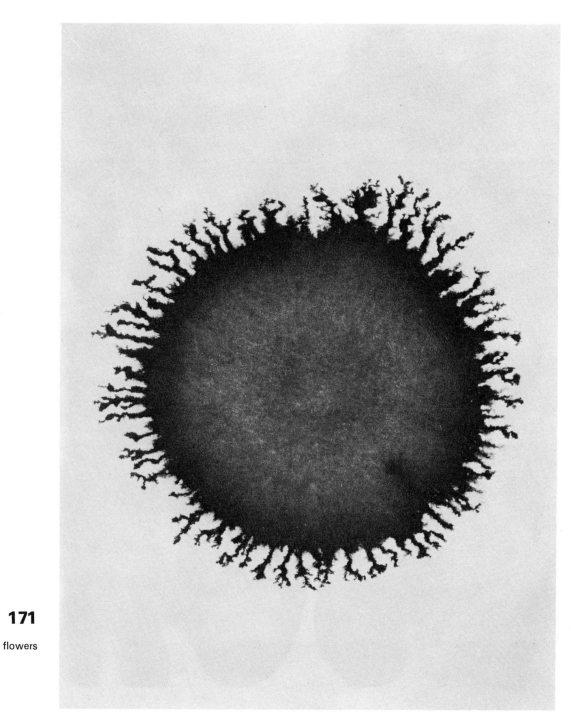

150. Enlargement of part of Design 149.

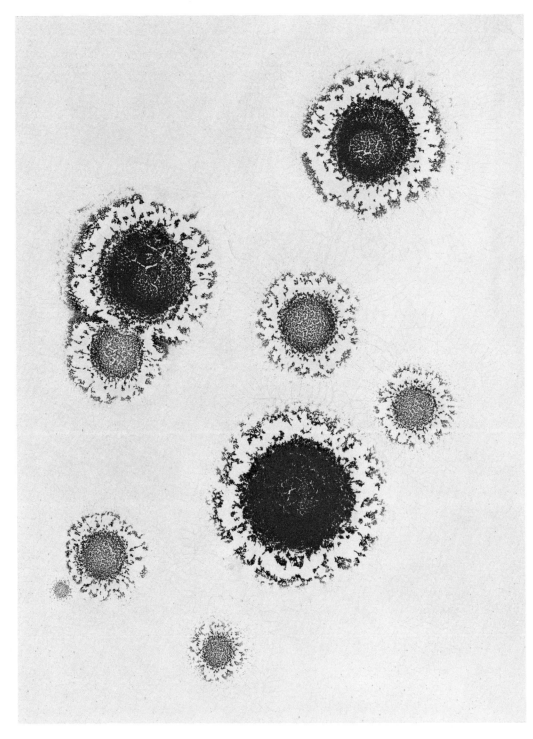

151. An illustration board panel is given a thick coat of white showcard color. While the paint is still wet, quickly place drops of a mixture of Grumbacher's powdered pigment and white shellac on the surface (6 parts of shellac to 1 part of pigment).

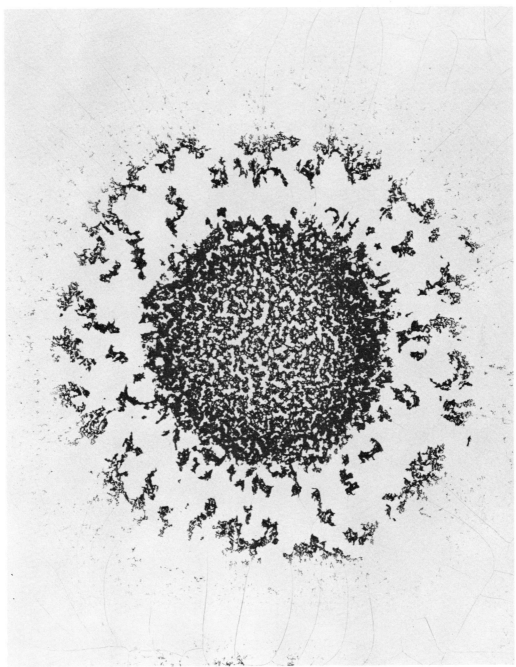

152. Enlargement of Design 151.

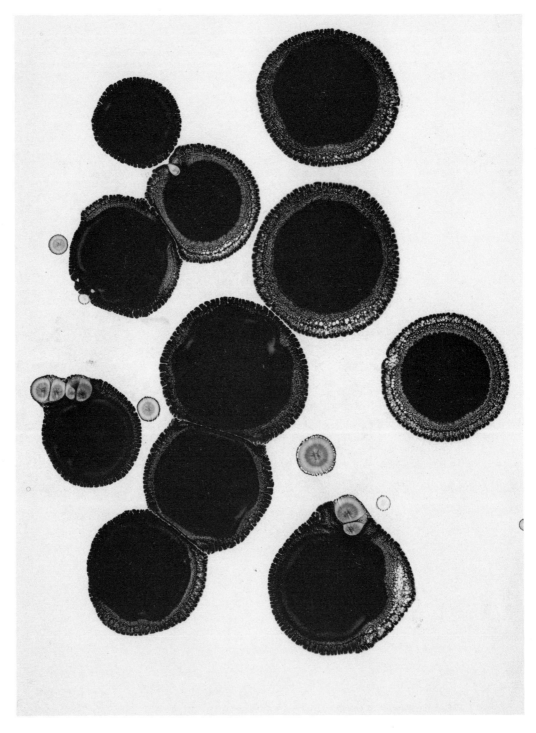

153. Coat the illustration board with white lacquer. Quickly drop on black lacquer, using a small brush or pencil dipped in the lacquer. Allow to dry.

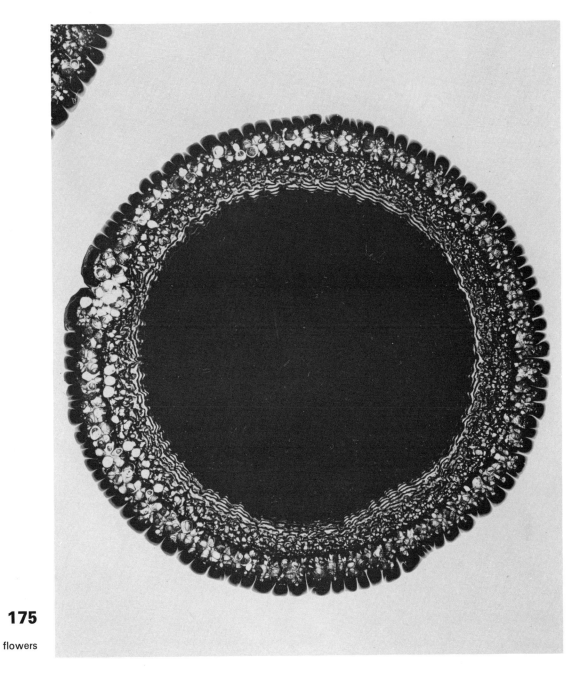

154. Enlargement of part of Design 153.

155. Cover the surface of the panel with well-mixed white Japan color. Lay the panel flat and quickly apply a few drops of black enamel to the still-wet surface. Allow to dry overnight.

156. Enlargement of part of Design 155.

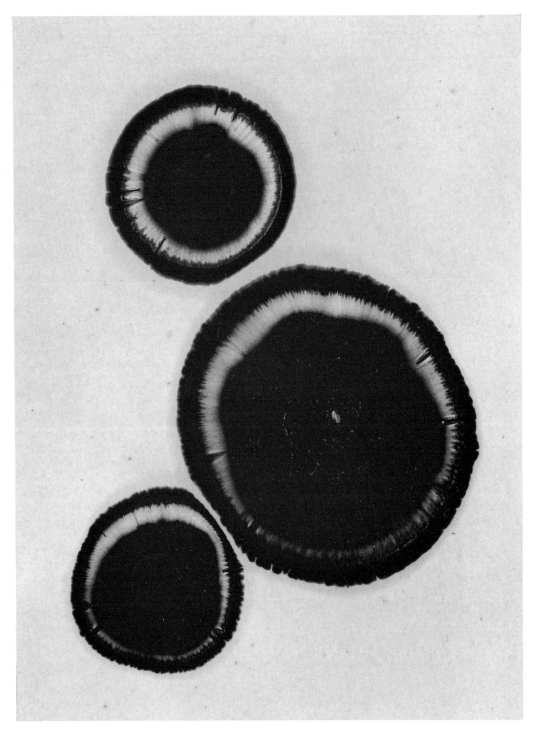

178

flowers

157. Cover the surface of the panel with a thick coat of clear lacquer. With the panel lying flat, quickly place a few drops of black enamel on the wet surface, dropping them from a stick or brush. Dry overnight without disturbing.

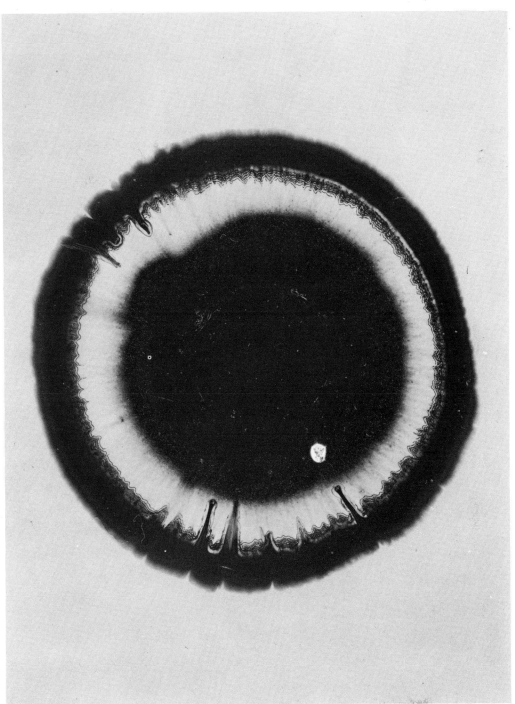

158. Enlargement of part of Design 157.

Fig. 49.

Fig. 50.

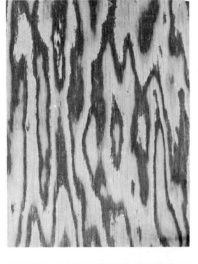

Fig. 53.

Fig. 52.

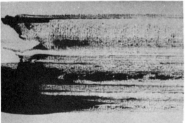

Fig. 55.

Fig. 51.

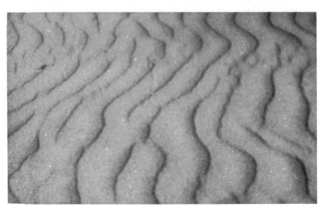

Fig. 54.

miscellany

The odds and ends of designs in this collection are not related in any particular way. Most of them could not be separated into categories large enough to warrant separate chapters. ■ Among them are "contour" designs made by allowing ink to flow into depressions in wrinkled paper, forming shapes very much like lakes or ponds in natural depressions in the earth. "Wave" patterns that appear on beach sand at low tide are duplicated in a water-filled baking pan. The flame of a kerosene lamp produces ghost-like images on a piece of white cardboard moved through the flame —images like x-ray films of some strange internal organs. In this miscellaneous collection of designs, it is difficult not to see images of real things.

> Sometimes we see a cloud that's dragonish;
> A vapour sometime like a bear or lion,
> A tower'd citadel, a pendant rock,
> A forked mountain, or blue promontory
> With trees upon't . . .
>
> Shakespeare, *Antony and Cleopatra*, ACT IV, SCENE 12

Fig. 49: Frozen mud puddle. □ **Fig. 50:** Contour marks in the sand. □ **Fig. 51:** Wind-made snow waves. □ **Fig. 52:** Island and lake designs: aerial view of coastline, Everglades National Park. National Park Service photo. □ **Fig. 53:** Wood growth-marks in plywood panel. **Fig. 54:** Sand waves. □ **Fig. 55:** Scrape marks on wall. Photos for Figs. 49 through 51 and 53 through 55 by author.

159. An illustration board panel is sprayed with alternating coats of white and black quick-drying enamel. Each coat is allowed to dry before spraying on the next. The panel is allowed to dry overnight and is then sanded with fine sandpaper, which reveals the various layers of paint in a contour-type design. The use of enamel in pressurized spray containers is the easiest and least messy way of applying a spray coat.

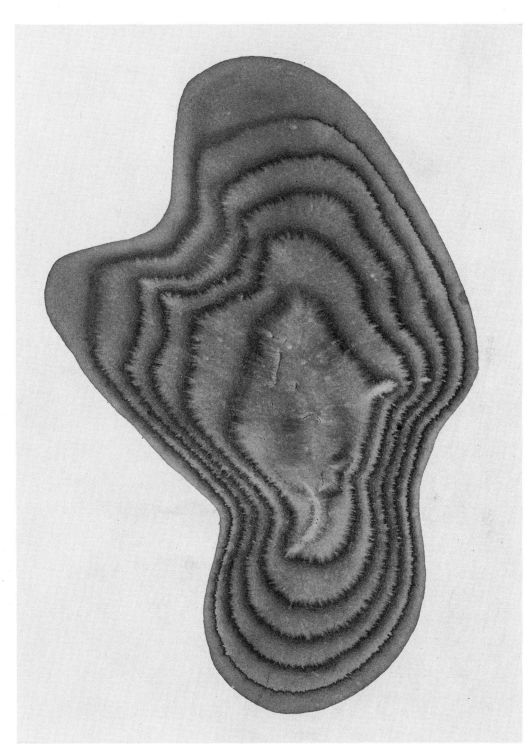

160. A water and ink mixture is prepared in the proportion of 40 teaspoons of water to 1 teaspoon of India ink. A piece of 2-ply Bristol board is bent into an irregular cone shape. The cone shape in the Bristol board is held in place with drafting tape or adhesive tape. The Bristol board is then placed on a support; the easiest way to support it is to use crumpled aluminum foil. Carefully pour the water-ink mixture into the center of the cone, taking care to avoid splashing. After letting it stand for 5 minutes, remove some of the liquid, using a plastic squeeze-bottle with a narrow top (the type used for applying wave lotion to women's hair). Allow to stand another 5 minutes. Again remove a portion of the liquid. Contour lines will appear at each level. Repeat until liquid is all gone. Remove the few remaining drops with the tip of a small brush.

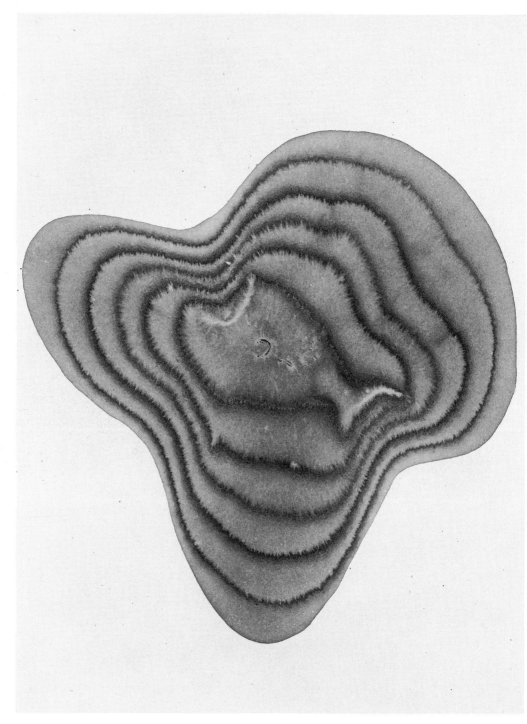

184

miscellany

161. Variation of Design 160.

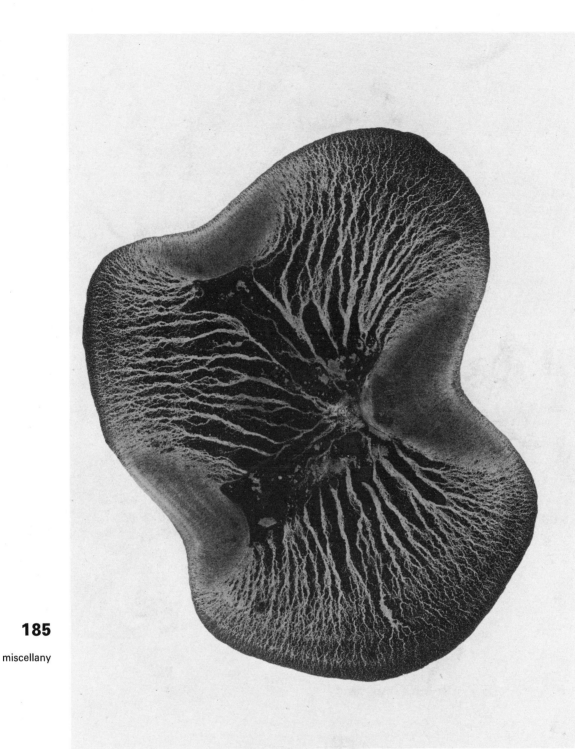

162. Follow the same procedure as for Design 160, but in place of the ink-water mixture substitute a mixture of black showcard color and water in the proportion of 20 teaspoons of water to 1 part of showcard color. Remove the mixture as quickly as possible with the squeeze-bottle, not waiting for the contour lines to form.

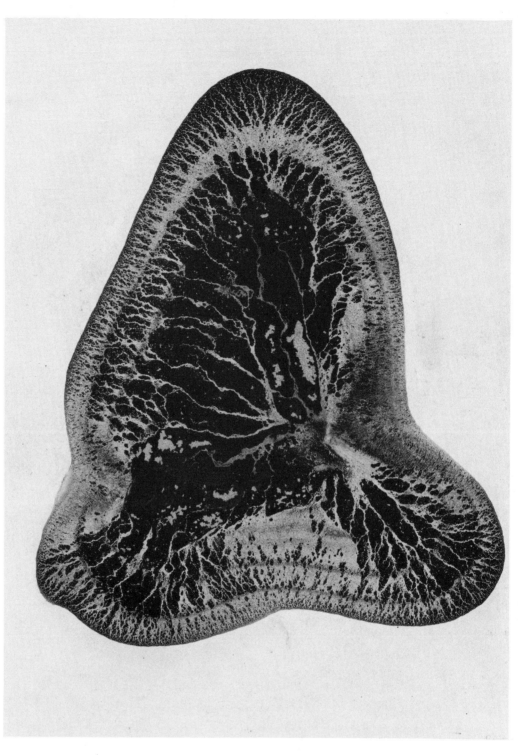

163. In this demonstration, time was allowed for the contour lines to form, but they are mostly lost in the complication of the flow lines.

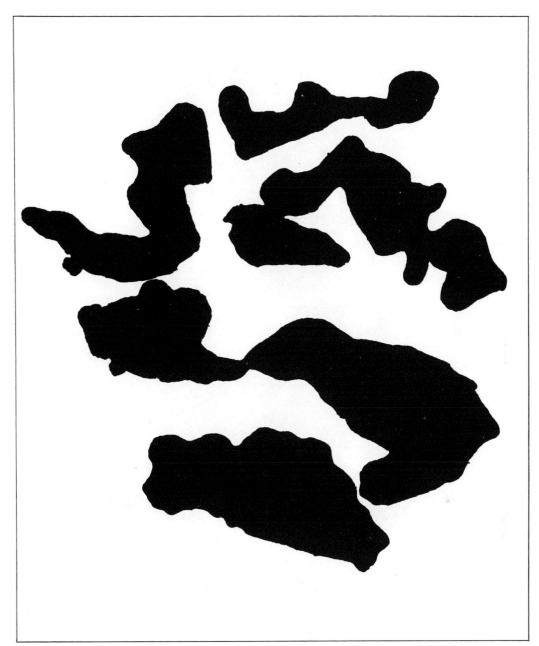

164. A piece of one-ply Bristol paper or ledger paper, 16" × 20", is crumpled into a ball. It is then "un-crumpled" and laid on a table so that the wrinkles are still well-defined, but the paper partially flattened. Place some black ink in a plastic squeeze-bottle that has a thin tapered nozzle in the cap (the type that is used for applying some types of wave lotion to ladies' hair). Squeeze some of the ink into one of the wrinkles in the paper. The ink will follow the "valleys" in the paper. Repeat in another valley. After the desired amount of surface has been covered, empty the bottle and use it as a syringe to remove the extra ink from the depressions in the paper. Allow to dry and mount.

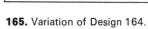

165. Variation of Design 164.

166. Variation of Design 165; reverse photostat.

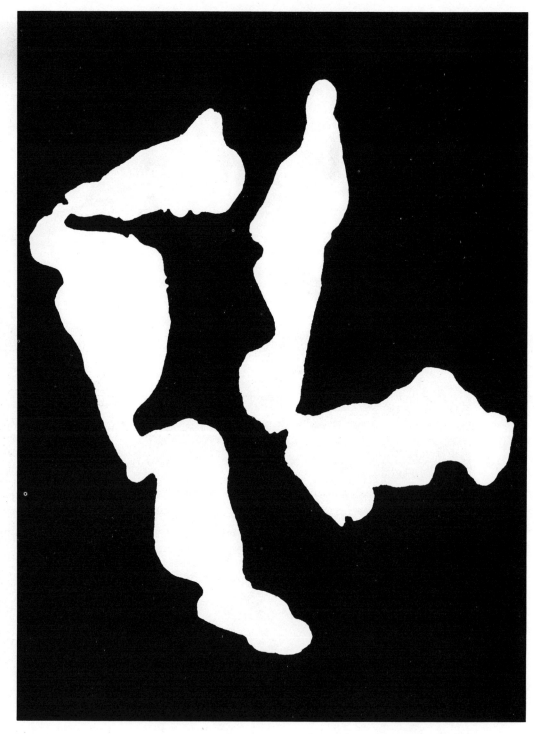

167. Variation of Design 166; reverse photostat.

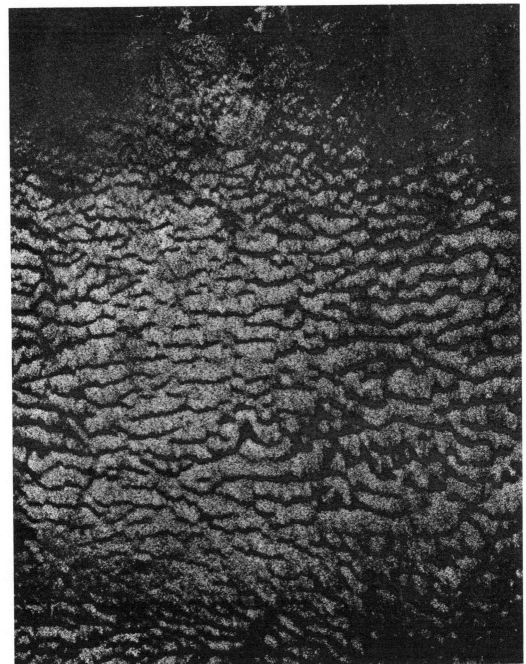

168. Place a 7″ × 9″ illustration board panel on the bottom of a 2″ deep baking pan, about 10″ × 14″. Tape the panel along the edges to the bottom of the pan. Fill to 1″ deep with water and sprinkle a teaspoon of powdered iron (obtained from a child's chemistry set) as evenly as possible over the surface. Agitate the water to make all the iron powder sink. Rock the pan gently from side to side, following the rhythm of the waves, until a well-defined pattern is formed on the panel. Use a rubber-tube siphon or syringe to remove the water carefully from the pan without disturbing the design on the panel. After the water has been completely removed, lift the panel gently onto some newspapers to dry overnight. Spray heavily with fixative to make the iron particles stay in place. After the fixative is dry, flow on a coat of clear lacquer with a brush to insure the permanence of the design.

169. Variation of Design 168.

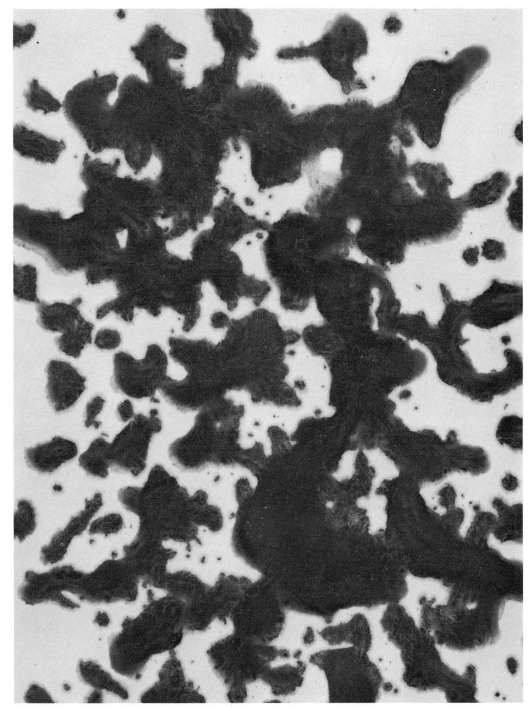

170. Remove the wrapper from a red-violet crayon (Crayola brand) and scrape the crayon lengthwise with a sharp knife, allowing the shavings to fall onto the surface of a white panel. An electric heat-lamp is held near the surface so the crayon shavings melt and form a pattern.

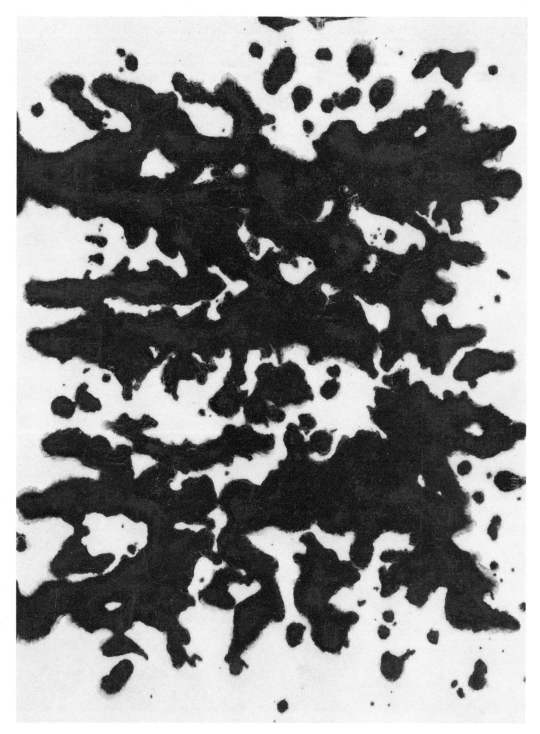

171. A variation of Design 170, using orange-red crayon.

172. Use two illustration board panels of the same size. Coat one of them with a heavy coat of rubber cement, then wait about one minute before pressing it flat against the face of the second panel. Immediately pull the two panels apart and allow the rubber cement on the second panel to dry. Spray with ink, using an air brush. Allow ink to dry; blot with newspaper and remove rubber cement by rubbing with the fingers.

173. Variation of Design 172. Wait for a slightly longer period before pressing the first panel against the second.

174. Tie a piece of ordinary white household string, 18" long, to the end of a pencil. Dip the string into black ink, removing enough of the ink from the string with a rag to keep it from dripping. "Flail" the surface of a piece of illustration board with the inky string, holding the pencil, and using it in the manner of a whip.

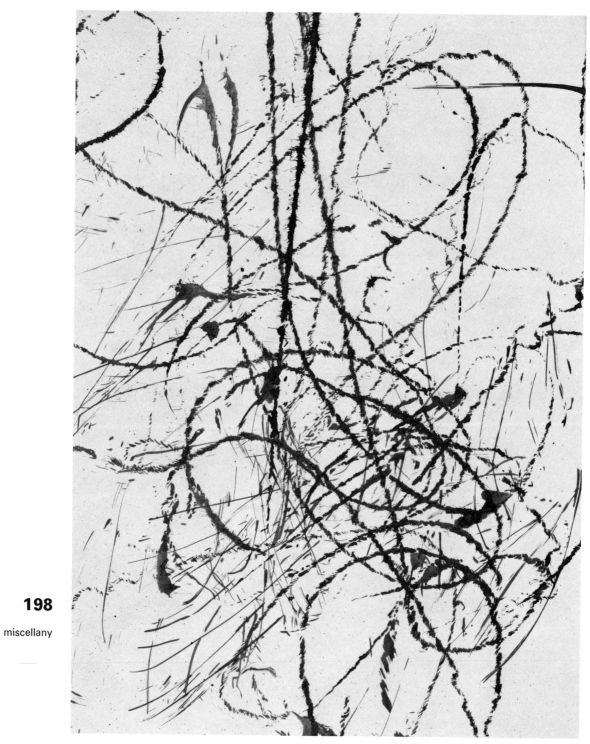

175. Variation of Design 174.

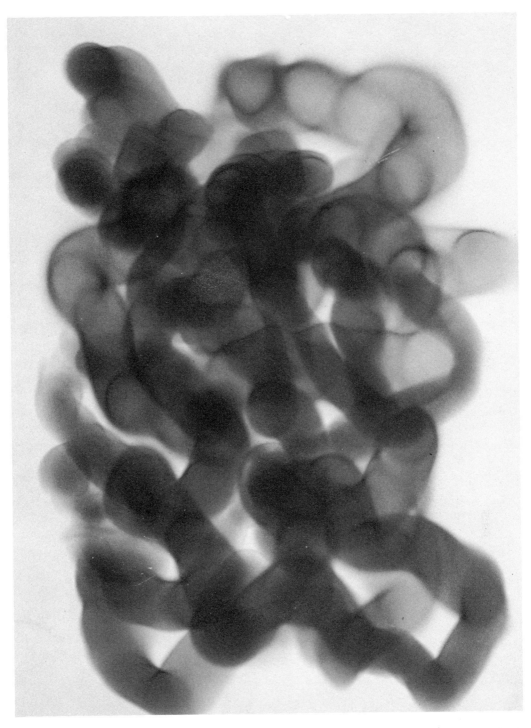

176. Hold the illustration board horizontally over a candle flame, close to the wick, so that the soot is deposited on the board. Move the board in an irregu- lar motion, watching the soot deposit until a desirable design is achieved. Spray with a fixative like Krylon.

177. Use the same procedure as for Design 176, but hold the panel at approximately a 45° angle.

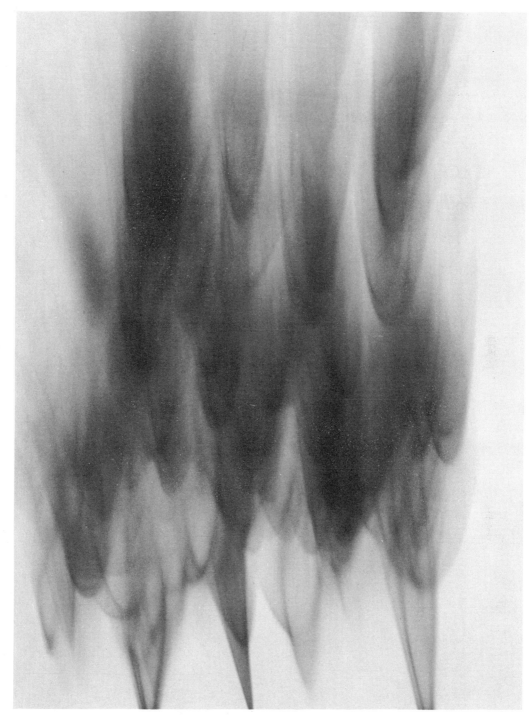

178. Hold the panel at a steep angle, almost vertically, to get this effect.

179. Black showcard color scraped off a white panel with a palette knife.

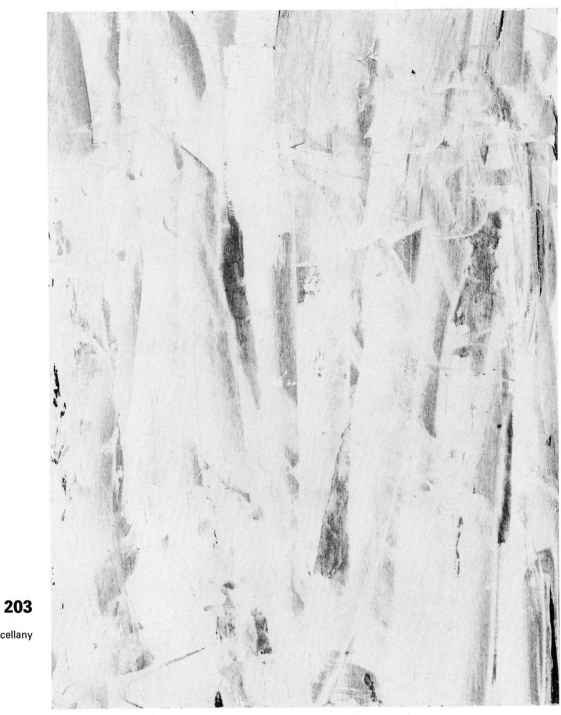

180. White showcard color scraped off a black panel with a palette knife.

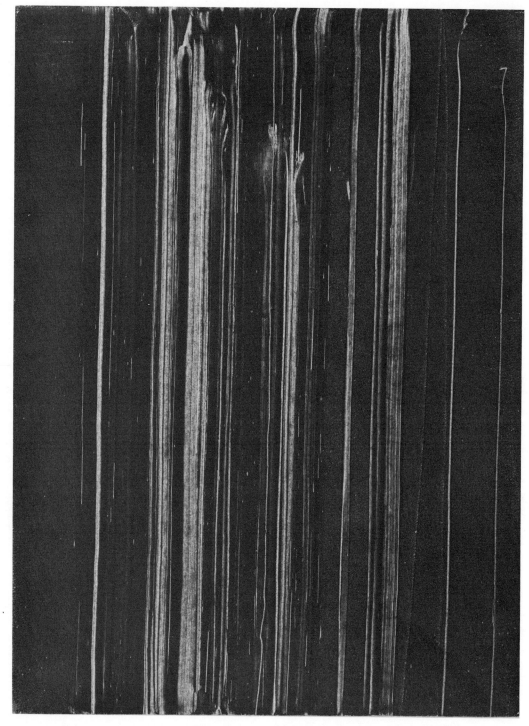

181. Using a brayer (rubber hand-roller), coat the surface of a piece of illustration board evenly with finger paint. Crumple a piece of ordinary typing paper and pull it carefully across the surface.

182. A scribble made with the finger, using finger paint.

183. A heavy coat of rubber cement is applied to a panel. After drying, place another clean panel on top of the rubber cement side and carefully rub the two panels back and forth for a couple of inches. The friction of the clean panel will cause some of the rubber cement to rub off, leaving some bare spots on the dry rubber cement surface. Spray with black ink and when dry, remove the remaining rubber cement by rubbing with the fingers.

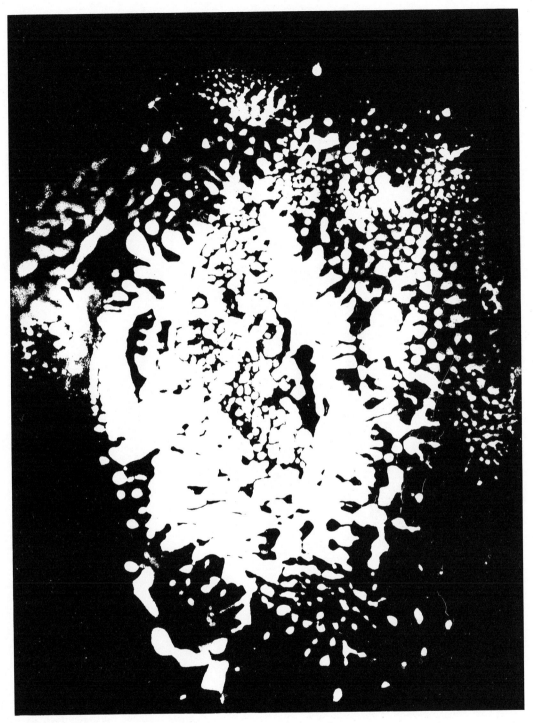

184. Brush a thick coat of white showcard color onto a piece of scrap cardboard. Just as the paint begins to dry, press a piece of black cardboard onto the painted surface. The wet parts will adhere in an irregular design.

185. Use a panel that has been sprayed with black gloss enamel. Stand the panel in a sink, at a 45° angle. Apply a mixture of white showcard color and water (6 parts water to 1 part paint). Add a few drops of detergent to keep the panel from rejecting the paint. Apply more paint-water mixture to the top edge of the panel and allow it to run down over the surface. Let stand in this position until dry.

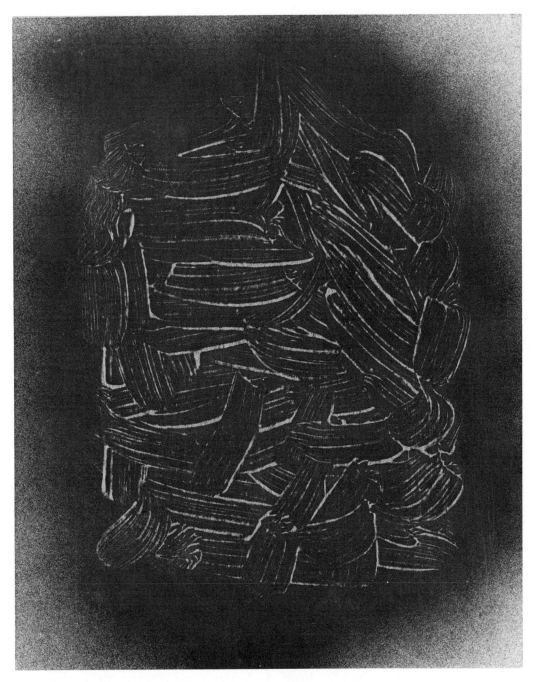

209

miscellany

186. Using a ½" brush, coat the surface of the panel with Grumbacher's MG Quick-Drying Titanium White. Allow it to dry for several days. Spray with black enamel. When it is thoroughly dry, sand lightly with very fine sandpaper.

materials
and equipment

The materials and equipment used in making the illustrations in this book are listed here. They were purchased in the Washington, D. C. area. Since many manufacturers market their goods in limited areas, some of the brands named will be unobtainable elsewhere, but there is no reason why substitutes will not do just as well. Because of variations in the composition of paints and inks, do not expect results *precisely* like those illustrated and do not be surprised if you experience an occasional failure. Other factors that also affect the design are temperature, humidity, and thickness of application. In the case of crayons, Crayola seemed to work much better than most; some of the other brands of crayons contain ingredients that prevent proper melting when used with a heat lamp. ■

Many paint and art materials present health hazards, and labels should be consulted for appropriate warnings. Lacquer, lacquer thinner, enamels, shellac, fixatives, rubber cement, oil paint thinners, and some household cements contain volatile poisons that should not be inhaled or come into prolonged contact with the skin. Many products in pressurized containers are also in this category. All of these materials should be used in a well-ventilated room, or better still, out of doors. By a well-ventilated room I mean a room with a noticeable current of air that quickly takes the fumes out a window or ventilating system. Another hazard in using these materials is the danger of fire or explosion, so the obvious precaution should be taken of avoiding heat, flames, and sparks.

Air Brush

Thayer & Chandler Model A: A simple and effective air brush, used for spray-application of transparent watercolor or opaque air brush colors. Is often used in photo retouching. Requires a compressed air or carbon dioxide supply along with hose, air gauge, and pressure regulator. [*Thayer & Chandler Company,* Chicago, Illinois]

Bristol Board

Bristol board is the term used to describe a type of heavy drawing paper that is widely used for ink drawings, lettering, and general artwork. Both sides are

210

usable. Bristol board comes in a smooth "plate" finish and in a medium finish that has a slight "tooth." It comes in several thicknesses, 1 ply being the thinnest, and successive heavier thicknesses being built up of two or more plies laminated together. Artists usually work on boards of from 2 to 5 ply. Sheets usually come in 22″ × 30″ size.

Bainbridge Studio Bristol: Comes in several thicknesses, 1 ply to 4 ply. Smooth plate finish, 2 ply, is very useful. [*Charles T. Bainbridge's Sons*, Brooklyn, New York]

Crayons

Crayola Crayons: Non-toxic children's crayons; come in many different colors, and melt at a temperature that is useful for the "accidental effects" described in the text. [*Binney and Smith*, New York, New York]

Detergent

Vel: A pink liquid detergent used for washing clothes and other household use. [*Colgate-Palmolive Company*, New York, New York]

Enamel

Enamels are manufactured in such a way that they make a harder, smoother, and glossier coating than paint. Brush marks tend to disappear when enamel is applied with a brush.

Duco "Spray Magic": Comes in pressurized containers, in many colors; types used in this book are Duco Gloss Black #440 and Appliance Gloss White #439. Can be used on wood, metal, cardboard. [*E. I. Du Pont de Nemours & Co.*, Wilmington, Delaware]

Super-Tex Odorless Enamel: Comes in black, white, and colors. [*Tex Products Company*, Newark, New Jersey]

Finger Paint

Amaco Finger Paint: Eight different colors, non-toxic. Works best on a non-absorbent surface. Finger paint papers are made especially for this purpose, but illustration board can be sprayed with clear lacquer or coated with shellac, and the paint can be used quite well on this surface. [*American Art Clay Company*, Indianapolis, Indiana]

Fixative

Krylon Spray Coating: A fixative in a pressurized spray container; for pencil, charcoal, pastel drawings. A permanent, clear acrylic spray. Comes in a clear, glossy finish and in a non-glossy finish that can be worked over with charcoal, pencil, etc. Should be used in a well-ventilated room. [*Krylon, Inc.*, Norristown, Pennsylvania]

211

Glue

LePage's Original Glue: A brown liquid glue for use on wood, leather, cloth. Wash brush or applicator in water. [*LePage's*, Gloucester, Massachusetts]

Elmer's Glue-All: A general-use white liquid glue for use on paper, wood, cloth, or other porous substances. Glue brushes can be cleaned with soap and water before the glue sets. Can be thinned with an equal part of water and used as a transparent coating. [*The Borden Chemical Company*, New York, New York]

Duco Household Cement: An all-purpose fast-drying adhesive for bonding china, wood, metal, leather, glass, paper. Use acetone or nail-polish remover to clean cement from fingers. Should be used with proper ventilation. [*E. I. Du Pont de Nemours & Co.*, Wilmington, Delaware]

Krylon Spray Adhesive: Pressure-sensitive adhesive in a spray can. It dries clear and quickly, and is water-resistant. [*Krylon, Inc.*, Norristown, Pennsylvania]

Miracle Black Magic Adhesive: A thick black adhesive in tubes. Binds metal, cement, brick, tile, glass. [*Miracle Adhesives Corp.*, Bellmore, New York]

Graphite

Microfyne Graphite "Lockmate": A fine graphite powder in plastic squeeze-type container, useful for lubricating. [*The Joseph Dixon Crucible Co.*, Jersey City, New Jersey]

Illustration Board

A standard material used by commercial artists; it is made of a sheet of good quality drawing paper mounted on stiff cardboard, one side only. It is manufactured with different paper surfaces, varying from very smooth to rough. Usually it is sold in either single thick (about $\frac{1}{16}$") or double thick ($\frac{1}{8}$"). Boards are sold 20" $\times$ 30" and 30" $\times$ 40".

Bainbridge Board No. 172: Single thick illustration board, 30" $\times$ 40". A good quality drawing board with a smooth surface for lettering, fine line pen and ink, air brush work. [*Charles T. Bainbridge's Sons*, Brooklyn, New York]

Crescent No. 201: Medium weight 30" $\times$ 40" good quality paper on stiff cardboard. [*Crescent Cardboard Co.*, Chicago, Illinois]

Ink

Higgins American Drawing Ink: Comes in 16 colors, black and white, in bottles with built-in dropper in cap. Colors are transparent and waterproof. For making colored drawings and transparent washes. Can be used in air brush. Black and white are opaque. [*Higgins Ink Co., Inc.*, Brooklyn, New York]

Marsh Felt Pen Ink: Black and seven colors. Comes in small oil-can type containers with screw-on nose on spout. Inflammable. [*Marsh Company*, Belleville, Illinois]

Pelikan Waterproof Drawing Ink: Comes in 19 different colors, black and white, in bottles with built-in dropper in cap. For transparent washes, colored drawings, air brush. Black and white are opaque. [*Gunther-Wagner, Kohinoor Pencil Company*, Bloomsbury, New Jersey]

"Snow White" Johnston's Special Grade White Ink: A white ink for pens, brushes, and air brush. Stir or shake well before using. [*Johnston's Snow White Products*, Rochester, New York]

Ink Pens

Leroy Lettering Pens: These small metal pens are designed for use with India ink, and are excellent for drawing lines of uniform width. The pens come in two parts; a lower "pen," into which fits a "cleaner." They are made in a variety of sizes. When employed for drawing lines they must be used with a Leroy Socket Holder that fits into any standard penholder. [*Keuffel and Esser*, Hoboken, New Jersey]

Iron (Powdered)

Can be obtained from a scientific supply company or children's chemistry set.

Japan Color

Japan colors are like oil paints, but instead of being ground in oil, the base is varnish containing driers. The material dries quickly to a dull matte finish, and can be used on paper without causing wrinkling. Japan color is often sold in tubes, especially to the signpainting trade, but some brands come already "thinned," in cans.

Skoler Display Art Flat Poster Colors: An already-mixed quick-drying Japan paint in cans. Waterproof paint that does not wrinkle paper. Black, white, and various colors. Thin with turpentine or oil-paint type thinner. [*Massachusetts Paint Company*, Springfield, Massachusetts]

Lacquer

Lacquer is usually sold in various colors, as a pigmented coating, but is also made clear and transparent. It dries completely by evaporation of the solvent, and is the fastest-drying finish.

Rogers Brushing Lacquer: Quick-drying lacquer, clear and in various colors. Should be used in a well-ventilated room, or preferably out of doors. [*Rogers Paint Products, Inc.*, Detroit, Michigan]

Baer Brothers Lacquer: Clear, or in various colors. [*I-SIS Chemicals, Inc.*, Springfield Post Office, Stamford, Connecticut]

Metal Foil

Reynolds Wrap: Aluminum foil in rolls, box-dispenser container. For freezing, broiling, and cooking foods; general household use. [*Reynolds Metals Company*, Richmond, Virginia]

213

Oil Paint

MG Quick-Drying Titanium White: A white oil paint in tubes. Dries more or less quickly, depending on the thickness of application. Its most useful quality is that it retains palette knife and brush marks and other textural effects. [*M. Grumbacher, Inc.*, New York, New York]

Pretested Permanent Oil Colors: Come in tubes, $1'' \times 4''$, more than 50 different colors, plus zinc white, flake white, titanium white. [*M. Grumbacher, Inc.*, New York, New York]

Paper

Color-Vu: This brand of colored paper comes in a set of systematically organized colors, printed on one side of the paper. In addition to the full-strength hue, each color also comes in four tints and three shades. There is also a series of gradated greys. Paper comes in two sizes: $18'' \times 24''$ and $24'' \times 36''$. [*Color-Vu*, New York, New York]

Paste, White

Carter's Liquid Paste: A liquid paste for use on paper. [*Carter's Ink Company*, Cambridge, Massachusetts]

Higgins White Paste: A thick white paste for use on paper. [*Higgins Ink Company*, Brooklyn, New York]

Pigments, Dry Powdered

Grumbacher Dry Color, Artists Color: Can be used in oil, casein, tempera, watercolor. [*M. Grumbacher, Inc.*, New York, New York]

Plastic Wrapping Material

Dow "Saran Wrap": A thin transparent plastic wrapping material in rolls, for food wrapping and other household uses. Comes in rolls, in box-dispenser. [*Dow Chemical Company*, Midland, Michigan]

Rubber Cement

Best-Test White Rubber Paper Cement: An adhesive for paper-pasting. Inflammable; should be used only with good ventilation. Thin with Bestine rubber cement thinner. [*Union Rubber & Asbestos Co.*, Trenton, New Jersey]

Shellac

Gleamax White Shellac: Wash brushes with denatured alcohol. [*National Solvents Company*, Washington, D. C.]

214

Showcard Color

Showcard colors are opaque watercolors, usually sold in 2-ounce, half-pint, and pint jars. They are widely used by commercial artists and signpainters. Showcard color is also known as *poster color* or *tempera*.

Crown Tempera Colors: Poster paint in black, white, and colors. Should be stirred well before using. Clean brushes in water. [*Iddings Paint Company*, Long Island City, New York]

Sodium Silicate Solution

This material is also known as "waterglass," and was used as an egg preservative before refrigeration became widespread. It is still carried by some drugstores and laboratory supply companies, and is sometimes found in children's chemistry sets.

Spraying Devices

Jet-Pak "Sprayon": This device can be used for spraying lacquer, ink, paint, or any other liquid that can be thinned to the proper consistency for spraying. It consists of a plastic housing, to which are fastened two containers: a small glass jar to hold the liquid to be sprayed and a can of pressurized propellent to provide spraying pressure. [*Sprayon Products*, Cleveland, Ohio]

Thinner, Oil Paint

Peerless Odorless Thinner: A clear thinner for oil paints, varnishes, and enamels. [*The H. B. Davis Company*, Baltimore, Maryland]

Tracing Paper

Albanene: A good all-purpose tracing paper that can be used for either pencil or ink. Comes in light, medium, and heavy weight. [*Keuffel & Esser Company*, Hoboken, New Jersey]

The Parchment: A medium weight tracing paper, useful for pencil tracing. [*Bienfang Paper Company*, Metuchen, New Jersey]

Wax Paper

Scott "Cut-Rite" Wax Paper: A heavy translucent waxed paper for food wrapping and other household uses. Comes in roll, in box-dispenser containers. [*Scott Paper Company*, Chester, Pennsylvania]

Water Color, Liquid

Dr. Ph. Martin's Water Color: "Synchromatic Transparent Watercolors." A liquid watercolor in small bottles. 39 different colors. Also has a liquid bleach for removing color from areas desired, after color has dried. [*B. Aronstein & Company*, Flushing, New York]

215